**From Surviving to Thriving
Mastering the Art of the El**

From Surviving to Thriving

Mastering the Art of the Elementary Classroom

Linda L. Carpenter, M. Ed.

Jennifer J. Fontanini, Ed. D.

Linda V. Neiman, Ph. D.

BRIDGING the Gaps in Education™
Lorenz Educational Press
P.O. Box 802 • Dayton, OH 45401
www.LorenzEducationalPress.com

Editor: Blair Bielawski
Book Design: Digital Dynamite, Inc.
Cover Design: Kate Kimble

© 2010 by Lorenz Educational Press, a Lorenz company

Permission to photocopy the reproducible materials in this book is hereby granted to one teacher as part of the purchase price. This permission may only be used to provide copies for this teacher's specific classroom setting. This permission may not be transferred, sold, or given to any additional or subsequent user of this product. Thank you for respecting copyright laws.

Lorenz Educational Press
a Lorenz company
P.O. Box 802
Dayton, OH 45401-0802
www.LorenzEducationalPress.com

Printed in the United States of America

ISBN: 978-1-4291-1960-3

v

Table of Contents

Introduction 1
Chapter 1: Rest, Reflect, Renew 5
Chapter 2: First Contact with Parents 16
Chapter 3: Partnering with Parents 33
Chapter 4: Engaging in School Culture 48
Chapter 5: It's About Time 57
Chapter 6: Space Strategies 71
Chapter 7: Building Relationships with Students 79
Chapter 8: Responding to Student Behavior 93
Chapter 9: Last Words, Next Steps 106

Bibliography 117
Appendix: CD Contents 121

About the Authors 125

Introduction

You do it because you know that's what will make a difference, because you believe that there's no such thing as a child that can't learn; that every child has their own gifts, and it's up to us to discover them, and it's up to us to see in our children what they can't yet see in themselves.

—President Barack Obama honoring Anthony Mullen, the 2009 National Teacher of the Year

The really good teachers are able to read a child's story and recognize the remarkable opportunity to help author that story. The really good teachers know how to script confidence and success onto the blank pages. They know how to edit the mistakes. And they want to help write a happy ending. Really good teachers know they have the ability to make a child happy or sad, to make a child feel confident or unsure, to make a child feel wanted or discarded. And students know when we care, when we care enough to read their stories.

—Anthony Mullen, 2009 National Teacher of the Year

The teacher is the single most important factor for learning in the classroom. It is the teacher who defines the learning experience for students. It's about you and the teacher you become. Becoming a master teacher is a deliberate, ongoing process. To master teaching, you must possess a strong desire for continual growth and learning since nothing about students is static.

The definition of "master teacher" is based on our personal beliefs about teacher effectiveness. These beliefs have been shaped by our own experiences as classroom teachers, learning specialists, technology integration specialists, staff development coordinators, and currently, teacher preparation professors. A master teacher is one who nurtures his or her capacity for growth and excellence in the classroom through inquiry and investigation. A master teacher seeks to learn about students, about instruction and assessment, and about parents and families. Learning is a continuous process that requires master teachers to develop practices that promote critical thinking and self-directed learning. Not only do they evaluate themselves as an ongoing, daily practice, they set time aside to review, critique, and revise curriculum, time use, resources, units, and lesson plans. Master teachers dissect their own practice and the impact they are having on students and on learning. They probe into complex and unique situations that occur in the classroom to gain perspective and find solutions. When these situations arise, the master teacher is compelled to seek information from colleagues, students, and recent educational research and literature.

Beginning teachers face myriad new experiences during the first year of teaching: working with parents, learning student names, and organizing a classroom for learning are just a few of the hurdles. Each new experience is an opportunity for growth and improvement. When beginning teachers move from surviving to thriving, they begin to see how the broader culture of our society impacts students, parents, and teachers. Typically, it takes three to five years to master the basics and move toward teaching excellence. *From Surviving to Thriving* and the accompanying CD are designed to help you move more quickly into mastery by providing the framework for tasks and dispositions that are part of a thriving elementary classroom community. Mastery starts with your desire to make the classroom a place for all students to learn and grow. Whether you are just starting on your career path toward being a master teacher or you've been teaching for ten years, *From Surviving to Thriving* will help you develop new strategies and complement your teaching.

Although *From Surviving to Thriving* is not a theory book, brief explanations and rationales are given to provide a context for the activities, strategies, and tools suggested. Each chapter begins with an anecdote from a teacher in the field followed by a brief introduction that describes the contents of the chapter.

Master teachers communicate with parents, build relationships in their school, and seek resources to enrich the learning experience (Chapters 1, 2, 3, and 4). They plan, organize, and create environments that allow for maximum use of time and space (Chapters 5 and 6). Finally, master teachers build a community in their classrooms by attending to learners' diverse needs (Chapters 7 and 8). The accompanying CD contains lists, letters, student activities, family activities, recommended literature, lesson plans, and PowerPoint presentations. Teachers can use the documents as they are or customize them for their classroom use. The CD gives teachers a starting place for many common documents and activities that master teachers use regularly.

Our professional work is motivated by the possibility that every child will have great teachers who ask critical questions of themselves and of the educational field (Chapter 9). Master teachers search for ways to make their classrooms more inclusive and work to develop socially conscious students. They value the contribution that students can make in the future and teach with that future in mind.

Chapter 1
Rest, Reflect, Renew

Who dares to teach must never cease to learn.

—John Colton Dana, American Librarian

Julie, Kindergarten Teacher

School has ended, and I can't believe how exhausted I am. I never could have imagined that 18 kindergarteners could have worn me out so much! As I reflect on the school year, I am amused by the fact that much of what I did right was just by chance. Some things I did really well. My classroom looked great, the stations I prepared for free time were a success, and I found my organization strategies worked. Still, I could improve on things such as communicating with parents, planning more enrichment strategies for my units, and bringing more resources into my classroom. There are so many more things to learn about teaching. I have a vague recollection of things I learned in college, but that seems so long ago.

I signed my contract last July and was given the keys to my classroom. Since I only had five weeks until the start of the school year, I busied myself getting my classroom ready. I put up bulletin boards and door decorations, prepared name tags and welcome banners, and organized the student mailboxes. What I did not know was there were other things I should have been doing to lay the foundation for a successful school year. This year I will use my summer differently.

Introduction

What Julie is beginning to see is that there is more to teaching than putting up bulletin boards and preparing materials. Now she sees a bigger picture that includes creating a positive learning environment; building relationships with students, parents, and staff; and extending her own knowledge base in content and pedagogy.* Julie is realizing that she can positively impact student achievement by perfecting her craft. Summer provides an opportunity to chart a course of action to prepare for a successful school year.

Master teachers use their time away from the classroom to rest, reflect, and renew. They slow down their pace of life and reflect on what went well during the past school year and what needs improvement. Then, they reinvent themselves over the summer to start fresh in the fall. Master teachers take time to take care of themselves, feed their intellectual spirit, and perfect their craft.

Master teachers make lists. They use notebooks, index cards, day planners, smartphones, or computers. The form of the organization doesn't really matter. What does matter is that they regularly record information regarding professional and personal tasks. Your lists will range from materials you need for your next lesson to thoughts on how to improve a lesson next year. During the school year, there will often be stretches where there is barely enough time to plan quality instruction and attend to daily details, so it is vital to maintain organized lists of things that need to be addressed during the summer or other downtime.

Checklist—Last Week of School (and weekly/monthly, as needed)

- ❏ Clean out classroom files and piles.
- ❏ Throw out old materials that have not been used for two or more years.
- ❏ Discard old and tattered wall posters, borders, and bulletin board papers. Keep your classroom looking neat and fresh.
- ❏ Make a list for the custodial staff of everything that needs repairing, replacing, and/or removing—broken desks, damaged window blinds, or tiring technology.

---

* A variety of individuals may fill the role of parent for your students. Grandparents, foster parents, stepparents, or other relatives might be a student's legal guardians. There may also be multiple families involved. You need to be sensitive to this issue, and it is part of your job to know the situation for each of your students. Throughout this book, we will use the term parent with the understanding that it refers to one or more individuals who fill that role for each of your students.

- ❏ Assemble student and teacher materials that need to be updated or revised.
- ❏ Make a list of resources necessary to create units and lesson plans that need enrichment.
- ❏ Write thank you notes to those students who brought gifts on the last day of school. Maintain a list of students and their home addresses for future reference.
- ❏ Write thank you notes to staff members.
- ❏ Construct a school calendar for the upcoming school year. Record dates for summer meetings and for the beginning of the school year.
- ❏ Mark the date when the final class lists of students, with their home addresses, will be available and whether it's online or in hard copy.
- ❏ Organize and clean out your computer files. Move documents into portable storage devices and organize them in folders by topic such as parent letters, team building activities, science units, math units.

If you keep organized lists and follow the suggestions above, summer becomes a time to replenish and renew your mind and body, a time to attend to professional and personal tasks. Over that second cup of coffee during that first week away from school, make two lists: one for personal tasks and one for professional goals.

Checklist for Summer—Personal

- ❏ Make appointments for yearly exams—medical, dental, vision.
- ❏ Schedule home repair and big cleaning jobs.
- ❏ Organize personal living space: closets, garage, basement, kitchen, and storage areas.
- ❏ Set dates to reconnect with family and friends.
- ❏ If you have children at home, make a calendar/plan for their summer activities.
- ❏ Make a plan for exercise—consider golfing with a buddy, walking with a friend, taking yoga classes, or working with a personal trainer.
- ❏ Make a plan for nutrition—visit a local farmer's market, take a cooking class, or just try some new recipes.
- ❏ Check out resources in your community—libraries, museums, organizations, new restaurants and shops, athletic facilities, nature centers, and parks.

- ❏ Volunteer in your community—this may even develop into a classroom service project.
- ❏ Treat yourself to a manicure, pedicure, and/or a massage.
- ❏ Lunch at a new restaurant or plan an evening with friends.
- ❏ Take in a baseball game or other sporting event.
- ❏ Join a book club—check out the library or local bookstores for clubs in your area.
- ❏ Plan a vacation. Whether it is two days or two weeks, plan time to get away.

Checklist for Summer—Professional

- ❏ Find out if any of your students have special needs. If so, read books and articles, ask colleagues for tips, and plan to meet with school specialists.
- ❏ Attend a workshop or conference related to your professional goals or a district initiative.
- ❏ Consider tutoring students in the summer. It brings in some extra money and provides an opportunity to practice differentiation with one student in one setting.
- ❏ Write a professional goal for the coming school year. Many schools require you to set yearly goals, so get a head start and allow ideas to percolate into a plan.
- ❏ Read a book that applies to an area in which you want to grow professionally, such as differentiation, learning styles, community building, content, and assessment techniques.
- ❏ Look for new children's or adolescent literature for the classroom library.
- ❏ Plan new bulletin boards.
- ❏ Connect with a mentor or a respected colleague. REPEAT OFTEN.
- ❏ Meet with a new teacher and see how you can help.
- ❏ Visit a teacher store for ideas. What can you make from materials you have at home?
- ❏ Make a list of supplies you will need and watch for Back to School and area garage sales. Don't forget to check out eBay, too.
- ❏ Make a list of ideas you generate over the summer. Carry a notebook with you.
- ❏ Schedule a meeting with the principal—just to touch base.
- ❏ Schedule meetings with resource teachers—just to see what's new.

Although the following checklist is designed for new teachers, it may also serve as a checklist for teachers who are changing assignments or taking new positions.

Checklist for New Teachers or New Positions

- ❏ Meet with the principal, a mentor, and members of your grade level team as soon as you have the job. They will be eager to meet you, too.
- ❏ Request textbooks, curriculum guides, unit/lesson plans, and lists of available resources and resource teachers.
- ❏ Request any additional materials and supplies connected to the teaching assignment that you will need before school starts, such as grade level supply lists, newsletters, upcoming events, and planned field trips for the coming year.
- ❏ Request a teacher handbook or contract that outlines your rights and responsibilities.
- ❏ Read your contract. If you have questions, ask Human Resources or a representative from the teacher organization.
- ❏ Schedule an appointment with Human Resources to make sure you know what you need to do to secure your benefits and carry out your responsibilities.
- ❏ Request a school and district calendar.
- ❏ Get your school email set up and obtain a copy of the school email policy.
- ❏ Ask about any software that can be downloaded to your home computer. Many schools have licenses that allow this practice.
- ❏ Start working on units and lesson plans for the first quarter.
- ❏ Plan your classroom setup. (See Chapter 6.)
- ❏ Plan and create bulletin boards.
- ❏ Put your management plan together. What are your expectations and what will you do to create community? (See Chapter 7.)

What Experts Say: New teachers need help. From day one, new teachers, largely on their own, are responsible for running a classroom and ensuring student learning. It is little wonder that 14% of new teachers leave by the end of their first year, 33% leave within three years, and almost 50% leave in five years. (Wiebke & Bardin, 2009, p. 34)

Checklist—Month Before School Starts

- ❏ Assess progress on the summer checklists. Consolidate and prioritize remaining tasks. Make an action plan for completion.
- ❏ Finalize and print the letter that will be sent home to your new students and their parents. Make copies of documents that will accompany the letter. (See Chapter 2.)
- ❏ Check with the school secretary about a school mailing to parents. Ask about including your letter in this packet. If that is not possible, prepare mailing labels or envelopes for the letter home.
- ❏ Plan lessons for the first week of school.
- ❏ Prepare handouts and material lists.

Checklist—Home Visits

Home visits are powerful tools for building relationships. Teachers can appreciate the environments their students come from each morning and return to each evening. Parents and students see the visits as an invitation to form a partnership. Home visits require a substantial amount of planning and time on the teacher's part. Check the resources at the end of this chapter for ideas and planning. Consult with other teachers who have conducted home visits for ideas and advice.

- ❏ Attend a workshop on home visits or work with an experienced teacher to prepare for home visits.
- ❏ Meet with the principal to share your plan before scheduling visits.
- ❏ Schedule visits. If a home visit is not possible, invite the parents to school or consider meeting parents at their workplace. Meeting at the public library is another option.
- ❏ Create a short agenda for the meeting. Plan a few questions to guide your discussion. Keep the conversation light.
- ❏ Introduce yourself—first and last name. Share something about yourself before asking parents questions about their family and themselves.
- ❏ If students will be part of the visit, plan some short activities for them, such as an activity sheet or coloring page.
- ❏ Remember safety. Make sure you have your cell phone and that someone knows your schedule and where you will be. Use common sense when visiting neighborhoods with which you are unfamiliar. Consider conducting visits with another teacher.

> **What Experts Say:** In promoting a partnership between parents and teachers, home visits provide the means for effective team problem solving, observing children in their home environment, and encouraging parent involvement. Effective home visiting furthers the mental, emotional, and physical health and development of the child by serving the whole family. (Michigan Department of Public Education, 1999)

Checklist—Week Before School Starts

- ❏ Visit school. Connect with the principal, secretary, and other teachers, especially those teaching the same grade.
- ❏ Start getting your classroom ready. Do a quick inventory of what is there and what is missing in the classroom. Meet with the custodian.
- ❏ Put up bulletin boards.
- ❏ Prepare student name tags for desks, lockers, and cubbies.
- ❏ Have lesson plans with materials ready for the entire first week of school.
- ❏ Make copies for the first week of school.
- ❏ Meet with the school nurse for a list of students with health issues.
- ❏ Meet with special education teachers, counselors, social workers, and other specialists with whom your students may be working. Make appointments to discuss students with special needs and make a plan to meet those needs.
- ❏ Meet with your grade level team. Plan for the school year. Clarify your role and responsibilities as a team member.
- ❏ Get your specials (art, gym, music, library) schedules and construct your daily schedule for the school week.
- ❏ Check your computer login to make sure you have access to the system.
- ❏ Obtain student login information.
- ❏ Acquire and prepare a grade book and a lesson plan book.
- ❏ Find out school policies regarding grade books and lesson plans.
- ❏ If your attendance and grades are completed online, make sure you are familiar with the system and any upgrades that may have been added over the summer. Check to make sure all your students are listed and that you have access to all features you need.
- ❏ Make sure you know the emergency plans for the school. Fire and tornado evacuation plans may change from year to year.
- ❏ Review your teacher handbook. Make sure you are aware of any updates or changes.

- ❏ Make sure you know the process for calling in sick and obtaining a substitute teacher, as well as returning after a sick day. Check the handbook for the number of sick days allowed and what those sick days cover, such as doctor's appointments, children's illness, personal days, etc.
- ❏ Get duty schedules (hallway duty, lunch duty, bus duty) and mark your calendar now for the whole year.
- ❏ Get the district and school master calendar and transfer it to your calendar.
- ❏ If you have invited students and parents to drop by, make sure you are ready to greet them and show them around the room.
- ❏ Have a digital camera available to photograph each student on the first day of school.

> **What Experts Say:** Research suggests a positive connection between routines and student behaviors and routines and time available for learning. (Evertson & Weinstein, 2006)

Personal Considerations—Week Before School Starts
- ❏ Plan nutritious lunches for the first week of school and shop for the items and ingredients you will need. This will save money and time and keep you focused on your health.
- ❏ Plan dinner meals for the first week of school. Shop for the ingredients now so you do not have to shop after school.
- ❏ Drink water. Consider a thermos, water bottle, or bottled water to keep in your classroom. Stay away from the soda machine.

Professional Considerations—One to Two Days Before School Starts
- ❏ Clear your schedule for the last two days before school starts and just enjoy the time off.
- ❏ Come early for staff meetings that will provide time to meet and connect with colleagues.
- ❏ Be sure to welcome new faculty and staff.
- ❏ If you are the new teacher, put a smile on your face and introduce yourself. Start making friends. If you have an assigned mentor, make contact. If not, ask your principal to pair you up with an experienced teacher.

- ❏ Remember that patience and flexibility are essential. There will be changes to schedules and sometimes even to class lists. Stay cool and calm.
- ❏ Save a few minutes to walk the hallways to connect with staff. (See Chapter 4.)

Professional Considerations—Day Before Students Arrive
- ❏ Arrive early, but leave on time.
- ❏ Make sure your classroom is inviting by having things such as music, fresh flowers, or a pet goldfish.
- ❏ Try air fresheners to scent the room. (Never use a candle though—this is too dangerous.)
- ❏ Post tomorrow's schedule on the board.
- ❏ Post lunch choices.
- ❏ Have age-appropriate directions on the board for students to follow as soon as they come into the classroom.
- ❏ Review your lesson plans and make sure all materials are ready.
- ❏ Make sure your classroom is READY when you leave.
- ❏ Plan what you will wear for the week. You won't even have to think about it when you get up each morning.
- ❏ Have your book bag or briefcase packed before you go to bed.

Professional Considerations—Morning of the First Day for Students
- ❏ Plan a few minutes of extra time to focus for the day.
- ❏ Greet everyone in the office and colleagues in the school. People will see you as a positive contributor to the school culture.
- ❏ Double-check that everything is ready.
- ❏ Have soothing, calm music playing.
- ❏ Spend a few quiet minutes in your classroom. Focus.
- ❏ Smile! Please do not wait until Thanksgiving. That will be too late to connect with your students.
- ❏ Most schools have a plan for the first day of school. In some schools, all students go to a common area for a welcome from the principal. Be sure you know the plan and be at your station.
- ❏ Greet students and welcome them into your classroom. Shake hands with every student.

Professional Considerations—After the First Day of School

- ❏ Review and give feedback on any papers you collected today.
- ❏ Post tomorrow's schedule and lunch choices.
- ❏ Review lessons and arrange materials for tomorrow.
- ❏ Make sure the room is ready for tomorrow.
- ❏ Check your calendar. What is scheduled?
- ❏ Write a short reflection. How did it go?
- ❏ Make a list of things that need follow-up.
- ❏ Stay focused and organized so you can leave school on time and enjoy your evening at home.

Professional Considerations—First Week of School

- ❏ Record observations for early assessment of students.
- ❏ Prepare lesson plans and materials for Week 2.
- ❏ Send a positive letter home with a summary of the week's activities and what will happen next week.
- ❏ Start working on your class newsletter.
- ❏ Reflect on what worked and what didn't work.
- ❏ Make notes for things you want to change for next year.
- ❏ Congratulate yourself on a successful first week of school!
- ❏ Renew your spirit. Plan something fun and relaxing for the weekend. It is important to get away from school and spend time alone or with family.

Resources

Get Off to a Smart Start (Scholastic):
http://www2.scholastic.com/browse/article.jsp?id=10623

Middle Web's The First Days of Middle School:
http://www.middleweb.com/1stDResources.html

National Education Association: http://www.nea.org/

The Parent/Teacher Home Visit Project:
http://www.pthvp.org/about.html

Teacher Visits Hit Home:
http://www.educationworld.com/a_admin/admin/admin241.shtml

Resource Tools and Tips for New Teachers (Scholastic):
http://teacher.scholastic.com/newteacher/

Essential Resources for Your Classroom (Scholastic):
http://www2.scholastic.com/browse/teach.jsp

Wisconsin Education Association Council (WEAC) Beginning Teacher Handbook: http://www.weac.org/Professional_Resources/New_Teacher_Resources/beg_handbook/welcome.aspx

Check out your state's professional organization.

Tutwiler, S. W. (2005). Teachers as collaborative partners: Working with diverse families and communities. Florence, KY: Routledge.

Chapter 2
First Contact with Parents

Parents, too often, become and remain a forgotten treasure.

—P. Greene and M. Tichenor, Educational Researchers (2003)

Freda, Fourth Grade Teacher

The fourth grade curriculum in my district is awesome, especially for social studies and science. However, throughout the school year I discovered that the resources needed to teach each of these curricular areas were not as rich or up to date as I expected. Of course, I had a textbook, but it was limited in its perspective and its appeal. What I needed were strategies that would help me differentiate and make my units come alive. This really became evident as I began planning the Nifty Fifty States unit. I shared my concern over the lack of ideas and resources with my colleague across the hall. He suggested that I contact parents to see if they could help. I crafted a letter and sent it out. Parents offered to make treats and decorate for the Nifty Fifty States party. While these offers were definitely welcomed, the reply that caught my eye was from a parent who had been a social studies teacher at the middle school. She shared materials and texts, and she offered to help me plan the unit. The unit turned out great, students benefited, and so did I. This parent was a great resource.

Introduction

Freda is learning what most first-year teachers eventually discover: Teaching requires a multitude of resources. She discovered that parents can be resources to not only serve in traditional roles, but also to enrich the curriculum and classroom instruction. Typically parents volunteer to bring classroom supplies, snacks or treats, and help with parties or special events. But bringing parents into classrooms to serve as special guests, content experts, and small group instructors are effective ways to enrich the learning environment. Parents can contribute to the delivery of content and the practice of skills, ultimately impacting student achievement.

Effective teachers develop positive relationships with parents, in part, to tap into a multitude of resources. Teachers want to use parents to bring the outside world to the students. Parents have connections to people and resources that may enrich the classroom. Thus, parent resources can provide real-life experiences that make the curriculum more relevant and authentic.

Developing relationships with parents demands a deliberate process that may vary from parent to parent. Parents want to know who you are, what you value, and how you teach. Teachers want to know how parents can enrich classrooms and promote learning. Parents want to know how to contact you; what you will do to keep them informed of classroom activities; and the progress their child is making. This chapter provides a variety of ways to build partnerships with parents and stay connected throughout the school year.

> **What Experts Say:** When schools, families, and community groups work together to support learning, children tend to do better in school, stay in school longer, and like school more. (Henderson & Mapp, 2002)

Tools for Parent Communication

Letter to Parents and Students Before School Starts

It is essential to establish contact with students and their parents before the school year begins to lay the groundwork for a positive relationship. Master teachers send a letter home before school starts. The first letter home can set a warm, positive tone and invite parents and students to get to know the teacher as a real person. Most schools have student-management systems that include access to databases for personalizing mailings. Check with the school secretary or technology expert to learn about the tools available in your school.

Format for the First Letter to Parents and Students Before School Starts

Greeting
- Personalize the greeting.
- Mention the student's name within the body of the letter.

Content of Letter
- Introduce yourself as the student's grade level teacher.
- Share a little about your background and education.
- Include the essence of your philosophy of education.
- Ask parents to complete an attached questionnaire about their child.

Contact Information
- School email address.
- School phone and extension.
- Best times to contact you.
- Include an informal drop-in time for parents and students to visit before school starts. Include the specific date, time, and location. Be sure to clear this with both the principal and the custodian ahead of time.

Letter Closing
- Sign letter with first and last name.

Example of Before School Starts Parent Letter

August 1, 2010
Elmwood Elementary School
P.O. Box 123
Anytown, Wisconsin 55555

Dear Mr. and Mrs. Smith:

As Jacob's teacher for the upcoming school year, I am looking forward to getting to know you and to working with you.

I have been teaching for three years and have been at Elmwood Elementary school for two years. I am a graduate of State University with a degree in Elementary Education. Recently I have been learning more about differentiated instruction and assessment techniques.

All children are unique individuals with different interests and learning styles. We will be spending the first few days of school getting to know each other and discovering individual interests and talents. My goal is for our classroom to be a community of learners based on mutual respect for all individual differences.

Please share information with me about Jacob by completing the enclosed questionnaire so that I may begin to plan to meet his needs.

Throughout the year you are welcome to visit our classroom. Watch for information I will send home concerning volunteer opportunities and different ways you may support our classroom.

Enjoy the last few days of summer. If you have questions, please contact me (mesmith@elemschools.org or (444) 333-5555, Ext. 1111). The best time to reach me is between 10:00 and 10:45 AM, Monday through Friday. You may leave me a voice mail message, and I will return your call.

I will be in my classroom working on August 21, 9:00 AM to 3:00 PM. If you and Jacob would like to stop in for a few minutes to say hello, please do so. Jacob may also drop off his school supplies that day. (See enclosed list.)

Sincerely,

Mary Smith
Grade 3
Elmwood Elementary

Example of Before School Starts Student Letter

August 1, 2010
Elmwood Elementary School
P.O. Box 123
Anytown, Wisconsin 55555

Dear Brett:

Wow! It is almost time to go back to school. I hope you had fun over the summer. I am very excited about the new school year; How about you?

This summer, I visited a real archaeological dig at the Anasazi Heritage Center in Delores, Colorado. Wait until you see the books and pictures I brought back. Learning about Native Americans will be one of our units this year. One of the bulletin boards in our room will be filled with pictures I took at the dig. Look for it when you come into the classroom.

Another bulletin board is reserved for you and your classmates. Please bring a photo or drawing of yourself doing something over the summer. We will post all the pictures and learn about everyone's activities as we get to know one another.

I also read several new books this summer. Did you have a chance to read a good book? I will bring one of my favorite books to share. If you have a favorite book, bring it to class the first week and share it with us.

I am enclosing the Supply List for Third Grade so that you will know what to bring on the first day of school.

It will be enjoyable to get to know each other. Our classroom will be a place you like, a place you feel safe, and a place where you will learn AND have fun.

See you soon.

Your new teacher,

Mrs. Smith
Grade 3
Elmwood Elementary

Example of Before School Starts Student Postcard

Message

Hi Brett,
 	
    I will be your new teacher for third grade this year. Right now, I am in Colorado learning about the Anasazi. They were the ancestors of the modern Pueblo people.
 	
    I have really cool information to share with you. Enjoy summer.
 	
See you soon.
Mrs. Smith
	Brett Student
	1234 Street
	Anytown, Wisconsin 55555

Front of Card

Parent Questionnaire

What to Include
- Contact information (parent name, email address, and phone number)

What to Consider
- Limit the number of questions to seven.
- Balance positive and negative questions and start with positive questions.

Questions to Consider for Parent Questionnaire
1. What are your child's interests?
2. What would you like me to know about your child?
3. What are your concerns about your child?
4. What is your child's attitude toward school?
5. What has been helpful for your child in the past?
6. How does your child learn best?
7. What additional school help do you believe your child needs?
8. Are there any changes in your child's behavior that concern you?
9. Explain any health problems your child has that may impact on his or her school performance.
10. Identify any family stressors that you believe may have an impact on your child's school performance, such as new baby, death in family, recent move, job loss, new job, new member of the household, and separation/divorce.
11. What are you child's strengths?
12. What are you child's weaknesses?
13. Would you like to schedule a conference to discuss your child?

Example of a Parent Questionnaire

Parent Questionnaire

Name of Student: _____ Nickname: _____

Parent/Guardian:

Name: _____ Relationship: _____

Email: _____

Home Phone: _____ Cell Phone: _____

Which do you prefer I use to contact you? _____

Parents play a vital role in children's academic and social progress. The information you share will help me meet your child's needs.

1. How does your child learn best?

2. What is your child's attitude toward school?

3. What has been helpful for your child in the past?

4. Explain any health problems your child has that may impact his or her school performance.

5. Identify any family stressors that you believe may have an impact on your child's school performance, such as new baby, death in family, recent move, job loss, new job, new member of the household, and separation/divorce.

6. What are your child's interests?

7. What would you like me to know about your child?

From the resource CD of *From Surviving to Thriving*. The original purchaser has permission to reproduce this page for use in his or her classroom.
© 2010 Lorenz Educational Press, a division of The Lorenz Corporation. All rights reserved.

First Week of School Letter to Parents

- Have a letter ready to send home to parents at the end of the first week of school.
- The letter should briefly summarize the activities of the first week of school.
- Include a family homework assignment that is easy and fun to complete.

Example of First Week of School Letter to Parents

September 4, 2010
Mrs. Smith's Third Grade Classroom—The Eagles
Elmwood Elementary School

Dear Families:

We just completed an awesome week of learning and connecting. There are 24 students in our classroom, and we should all know at least one interesting thing about each other. Ask your child to tell you about our community.

We chose a mascot for our classroom. We are the eagles because they are strong and show great courage. We plan to soar to great heights this year.

Together we agreed on some important norms for our classroom. Attached to this letter you will find our class Bill of Rights, which we created together. You will notice that all of us signed the document. We all pledge to do our best and respect the rights of everyone in our class.

Please take some time to talk to your child about school. Check your child's assignment notebook for information about next week or check our class Web page at http://www.classroom.org. Remember to refer to the Family Handbook when you have questions.

Our first newsletter will come home next Thursday in the weekly Thursday folder. Remember to check this folder each week.

Please contact me if you have any questions or concerns.

Have a great weekend.

Sincerely,
Mrs. Smith

Help Wanted Survey

Parents can assist the classroom teacher beyond providing cookies and chaperoning fieldtrips. Invite parents to complete a Help Wanted Survey that lists unique ways they can get involved.

Distribute the Help Wanted Survey by:
- Sending it home the first day of school or with the first class newsletter.
- Calling parents and conducting the survey over the phone.
- Distributing the survey during informal visits with parents and students before school starts.
- Presenting it during the first Open House and collecting it before parents leave.

What Experts Say: "As parent involvement increases, teachers experience rates of return on homework and develop a greater sense of efficacy and higher morale. They report more success in their efforts to influence their students." (Epstein, 2005, p. ii)

Example of Help Wanted Letter to Parents

Dear Parent or Guardian:

Parent involvement is an important ingredient in your child's academic and social success. You are an important part of our classroom. I would like to offer a variety of ways for you to be involved. Even if your work commitment makes regular visits to the classroom difficult, there are many ways you may contribute. Please check all that apply.

- ❏ Speak about your job or career.
- ❏ Share classroom-related pictures and souvenirs from a personal or family trip.
- ❏ Direct a play.
- ❏ Teach students to play chess or other board games.
- ❏ Arrange for curriculum-related speakers, exhibits, demonstrations.
- ❏ Share a talent, interest, or hobby.
- ❏ Tutor individuals or small groups of students or listen to students read.
- ❏ Mentor a student interested in your profession.
- ❏ Help publish books or classroom newsletters.
- ❏ Set up and help maintain a school or classroom Web site.
- ❏ Manage a classroom project.
- ❏ Chaperone a field trip.
- ❏ Organize or participate in a special event.
- ❏ Translate notices, letters, and forms into another language.
- ❏ Provide another parent with transportation to a conference or school event.
- ❏ Babysit for other parents on conference days.
- ❏ Donate books, art materials, musical instruments, games—whatever you think is appropriate.
- ❏ Bring in refreshments. Check with me for student food allergies.
- ❏ Prepare school materials at home.
- ❏ Other _____

Name: _____
Email: _____
Phone: _____ When can you be reached at this number? _____

From the resource CD of *From Surviving to Thriving*. The original purchaser has permission to reproduce this page for use in his or her classroom.
© 2010 Lorenz Educational Press, a division of The Lorenz Corporation. All rights reserved.

Contact with Parents

Phone Contact

We can't stress enough the value of positive communication with parents. Do your homework before you make the call. Know the parent's name—which may not be the same last name as the child's—and use the parent's name in the conversation. Use Mr., Mrs., Ms., or another appropriate title until the parent gives permission to use his or her first name.

- **Just Because—Positive Phone Calls**: Make it a goal to call each parent with a positive message concerning the student. You might want to begin the first week of school and make two to three calls each week until you have called all the families. Then, just start over. Make the message brief, positive, and specific to the student.
- **Calls of Concern**: As soon as you notice something different about a student or when you are concerned about student behavior or achievement, call home right away. Parents can't help when they are not informed.
- **Courtesy Calls**: Call parents who were not able to attend a scheduled school event and share whatever information they may have missed. If necessary, be ready to send home a special packet.
- **Leaving Messages**: If parents are not home, leave your contact information and a courteous request to return your call or try again later. Do NOT leave specific messages on voice mail or answering machines. You have no control over who will hear (or not hear) the message.
- **Who to Call:** Be sure to call all parents who may be involved in the student's life. Parents may have shared custody, so you may need to make two phone calls for the same student.

Email

Embrace the 21st century! Invite parents to communicate with you via email. However, do not make the assumption that all parents have access to email. Invite those who have email to use it; provide a system for communicating with those who do not have email or choose not to use it.

- Invite parents to send an email in the initial letter sent home. This will give you a correct and current email address for the parent, and you will know that email is an option for them.
- Invite parents to email feedback about a school event.
- Create a distribution list for open email communications with all parents.
- Use email to send newsletters, general announcements, updates, and reminders.
- Use email to answer parent questions.
- Use email to set up meetings with parents.
- Create a subject line that indicates this is a school email and the type of information included. For example: Name of the school and a key word (Lincoln Third Grade Newsletter or Lincoln Fourth Grade Reminder).
- DO NOT use email to inform parents of student issues or problems. Always meet with parents in person regarding sensitive student issues.

Web Sites

Many school districts provide teachers with Web pages and specific guidelines for Web site content and use. If this is available, make use of this excellent resource.

- Post contact information and times available to communicate and meet with parents.
- Post assignments. If possible, post assignments for the week to save time. Inform parents that this will be available when students are absent from school. Include guidelines and resources for current projects.
- Post activities for students and their families to do that connect to current topics.

- Post family handbook.
- Post upcoming events, units of study, school events, class events, and reminders.
- Post your weekly/monthly newsletter; send home hardcopies only to those without Internet access.
- Post resources, book and magazine lists, and Web sites for parents and students to use.
- If your school has home access to online subscriptions to databases or encyclopedias, share the access information with parents.
- DO NOT include names of students or parents on your Web page.
- If you post pictures, DO NOT identify students with names. Follow the district guidelines for posting student pictures. Some districts allow parents the opportunity to opt out of district postings. Make sure you honor that request.
- Know and follow your district web guidelines.

Family Handbook

A Family Handbook is a ready reference with information to answer many questions about the classroom and how it operates. It might include:

- Contact information and teacher availability
- Teacher philosophy of education
- Classroom procedures
- Classroom communications
- Classroom expectations
- Classroom norms
- Events, parties, and birthdays
- Curriculum topics
- Grading and homework policy
- Anything else you think parents need to know

What Experts Say: Students with above-average parent involvement had academic achievement rates that were 30% higher than those students with below-average parent involvement. (Henderson & Mapp, 2002)

Recordkeeping Tip

Maintain a paper log or a digital log of all communications you have with parents. This includes letters, emails, newsletters, personal correspondence, and phone calls. Documentation is useful and sometimes necessary. The trick is to create a system that is easy for you to maintain and easy to reference if you need it.

Communication Record

Date	Student/Parent	Reason for Communication	Outcome/ Follow-Up	Parent's Response

Date: Record the date you contact a parent, either in a digital log, paper log, or even in your personal calendar.

Student/Parent: Include both the student's name and the parent with whom you had the contact.

Reason for Communication: Indicate the type of communication and the specific reason for the communication—be brief but descriptive.

Outcome/Follow-Up: Indicate the outcome of the communication and whether or not you need to follow up with an additional action or communication.

Parent Response: One or two words can suffice to indicate the parent's response, which may help later with future communications.

Communication Essentials: Proofreading

- The best way to proofread is to read aloud. You will automatically catch errors in grammar and/or meaning.
- Ask someone you trust to read your writing aloud to you. You will hear how someone else perceives what you wrote and catch any mechanical errors.
- Use Spell/Grammar Check with everything, but don't trust these programs to catch all mistakes.
- Sending something to parents or school personnel that includes mechanical errors is unforgiveable and avoidable. Proofread, proofread, proofread.

Referencing Students and Parents

- Be consistent with your language. If you use *child*, use the word *child* throughout the document. If you use *student*, use *student* throughout the document. You may want to avoid using the words *sons* or *daughters,* since the guardian may be a grandparent, foster parent, or relative.
- The term *parent/guardian* is acceptable. However, using the name of the child's parent or guardian is preferable.
- One alternative is to write: *To the Parents/Guardians of Sally Student.* Using the student's name avoids mistaking the child's last name for the parent or guardian's last name.

Message Content

- Less is more. Determine the purpose of the communication and focus on that purpose.
- Communications should be limited to one page and easy to read. (Use a 10- to 12-point font size.) Make sure important information is easy to ascertain.
- Use everyday language. Avoid educational jargon.
- Date the communication.
- Double-check that all dates, times, and locations within the communication are correct.

Format of Communications

- Establish a standardized format for parent communications so parents know immediately how to respond to the communication. This might include different types of headings, memo formats, or fonts.
- Use different colored paper for different purposes. Yellow might be used for an update—no action required. Pink might indicate an upcoming event—mark your calendar. Green might require an action—sign and return.

What Experts Say: When teachers make parent involvement part of their regular practice, parents increase their interactions with their children at home, feel more positive about their abilities to help children in the elementary grades, and rate the teachers as better overall. The result is that students improve their attitudes and achievement. (Epstein & Dauber, 1991)

Resources

Class Handbook Resources
http://cmweb.pvschools.net/~skirby/S00C4226C.6/classroom%20handbook%2008.pdf

http://ms094.k12.sd.us/classroom_handbook.htm

http://www.stcharlesbloomington.org/sites/lolivera/a105.html

http://www.washington.k12.mo.us/schools/campbellton/staff/lengelbrecht/classroomhandbook.html

http://5088.educatorpages.com/Page.aspx?p=5088

Newsletter Resource
http://www.teacherweb.com/IN/WilliamsportElementary/Rickey/photo1.stm

Resources for Working with Parents
Communicating with Families (Scholastic):
http://www2.scholastic.com/browse/collection.jsp?id=337

Chapter 3
Partnering with Parents

Parents must acknowledge that the schooling that will be best for their children in the 21st century must be very different from the schooling they experienced themselves.

—**Andy Hargreaves and Michael Fullan, Educators**

Corey, Third Grade Teacher

About halfway through my first parent/teacher conferences, I began to breathe normally. It looked like things were going to turn out okay—in fact, better than okay. The parents were positive about the classroom and how their children were learning. Luckily, I had put some effort into getting ready for the conferences. I had decided on a mini-agenda for each conference, prepared a handout with classroom information for parents, and collected samples of each student's work to share with parents. One surprising outcome of the conferences was that many parents volunteered to lend a hand. Other than having parents sign up for snack days and field trips, I had not thought about how to involve parents in their children's education. Moreover, I was a little nervous about involving parents. Parents might see my inexperience as a limitation. However, overcoming my fears could result in having parents become an invaluable resource that would ultimately enhance classroom learning.

Introduction

Corey is moving beyond surviving the school year to realizing the potential that exists by partnering with parents. Connecting with parents has many benefits: content expertise, small group instruction, classroom organization, and special events. Anytime teachers invite others into their classrooms, they open themselves to new ideas, rich experiences, and feedback. Having parents in the classroom can be intimidating for some teachers, but the positive dimension they contribute makes up for the fear factor.

Master teachers are aware of how children develop socially, physically, psychologically, and cognitively. They seek information about students from multiple sources, including parents, and use it to plan developmentally appropriate instructional strategies and assessment techniques. Teachers learn about students and their families as they build relationships with parents. Master teachers understand the intimate connection between family, instruction, and learning.

What Experts Say: If we are to reach our goal of producing successful students, we must partner with the people ultimately responsible for those students—their parents. Develop and foster such a partnership. (Educational World, 2009, para. 4)

School-Wide Events for Parents

School-wide events foster and build relationships with parents. Back-to-School Nights provide opportunities for parents to visit classrooms and meet teachers, administrators, and support staff. In preparing for back-to-school nights, plan activities that mirror a typical day in the classroom. This may be the first meeting with many parents, so present a positive and energetic demeanor. Make a personal connection by greeting parents at the door with a smile and a handshake. Consider the following suggestions.

- Provide multiple invitations and reminders (class newsletter, email, assignment notebook, and Web site).
- Dress professionally—business attire is appropriate. (Dress the way you did when you applied for your job.)
- Invite parents to sit at their children's desks; however, also provide adult seating.

- Place letters that students wrote to their parents on students' desks.
- Encourage parents to leave a note or letter for their children to find the next morning. For students whose parents could not attend the event, write them a note yourself.
- Make sure your classroom is clean and ready for inspection.
- Create bulletins boards that showcase pictures of students working in the classroom during the first days of school.
- Post the daily schedule.
- Provide an activity for parents that is used with students.
- Use available technology. If an interactive white board is available, for example, use it for the presentation.
- Create a PowerPoint show to guide your presentation. (See PowerPoint Presentation for Parent Information Night on the CD.)
- Provide a one-page informative handout. (See the PIN Handout on the CD.)
- Share classroom expectations and norms. If students created a classroom Bill of Rights, share that with parents (see Chapter 7).
- Provide an overview of the curriculum.
- Share class, building, and district goals.
- Explain homework and grading policies.
- Offer suggestions for ways parents may support their children's education.
- Describe interactive parent homework assignments and explain the purpose of these types of assignments. (See examples later in the chapter.)
- Distribute Help Wanted parent applications.
- Assign parents homework. Give them a business card with your contact information. Invite parents to email comments about the evening; you will get valuable feedback and correct contact information, which you can then save to an email address book.
- Allow time during your presentation for general questions. Parents with specific questions should schedule a conference. Provide the best times to talk or meet with you.
- Remind parents that special area teachers are available to meet with them.
- If your school does not provide childcare during school events, consider suggesting it to the principal.

Events for Parents and Children—Open House

Open House is a wonderful time for students to showcase their classroom and their learning. Involve students in the planning process and prepare them to be ambassadors and guides for their classrooms. Showcase student work from current lessons and projects, making sure each student has an equal number of work samples displayed. Following are suggestions to make Open House memorable for parents and students.

- Include invitations and reminders in class newsletters, emails, assignment notebooks, and the class Web site.
- Start planning for Open House from the beginning of school by collecting student work samples.
- Select student work over time to show their progress in a content area—writing, math, reading, science, and/or social studies. This is an excellent assessment tool for the year and an impressive artifact for students to share with their parents.
- Train students to act as tour guides. With the students, prepare a short guided tour of the classroom. Allow students to practice the guided tour with each other and a staff member before Open House.
- Set up learning centers where students will teach their parents and siblings something they are learning in a specific content area. (See Learning Centers and Stations on the CD.)
- Plan enough activities to keep students and parents occupied for the time they are in the classroom.
- Talk to your principal about the possibility of providing transportation for families who might need it.
- Plan ways to include students whose parents cannot attend. Invite them in the day before or the day after Parent Information Night.

What Experts Say: Often teachers try to build a connection between family and the school by inviting parents into the building for events such as sports events, musical concerts, and classroom plays. They should also design instruction in which family members can be contributors in the learning process. (Werderich, 2008)

Events for Parents and Children—Family Nights

Family nights are school-wide events that get parents engaged and excited. A good way to educate parents about a particular content area or curricular goal is to host a family night with a content focus. These events require a great deal of organization from both faculty and parent volunteers, but they are well worth the effort. Participation in family nights provides another opportunity to build relationships with families and promote collaboration between families and school.

Events for Parents and Children—Family Math Night

One of the most popular family events is Family Math Night. Math Night gets students excited about math and provides an opportunity for parents to learn more about the math curriculum. More important, parents learn how to support their children's learning in math. There are extensive resources available, both in print and online, for Family Math Nights. Start with a group of committed volunteers and add to the pool each year with the goal of making Family Math Night a tradition at the school.

Resources

AIMS Education Foundation:
http://www.aimsedu.org/Activities/index.html

"Math Night by the Numbers" (Education World):
http://www.education-world.com/a_admin/admin/admin339.shtml

National Council of Teachers of Mathematics: http://www.nctm.org/

Stanmark, J., Thompson, V. & Cossey, R. (1996). *Family math.* Berkeley, CA: University of California.

Events for Parents and Children—Family Reading Night

Family Reading Night brings parents and children together for the sole purpose of sharing in the joy of reading. Work with a reading specialist at your school or district. Literacy is a national issue, and parents play a crucial role in the early development of literacy skills in young children.

Resources

The National Center for Family Literacy: http://www.famlit.org

National Institute for Literacy: http://www.nifl.gov/

Thinkfinity Literacy Network:
http://literacynetwork.verizon.org/TLN/

> **What Experts Say:** Collaborative family literacy intervention programs to improve the literacy skills of both parents and their children revealed significant increases in the amount of time parents read with their children, their enjoyment of reading time, and their use of specific parent reading techniques. Children have made significant gains in their enjoyment of reading with parents and their understanding of print concepts. (Weigal, Behal, & Martin, 2001)

Other Family Night Possibilities

Other ideas for family nights include nutrition/fitness, games, arts and crafts, science, and music/art. Below are resources that provide information for implementing family nights.

Resources

Free resources and planning kits for Family Nights are available from PTO Today: http://www.ptotoday.com/index.php

"Teachers Involve Parents in Schoolwork" (National Network of Partnership Schools, Johns Hopkins University):
http://www.csos.jhu.edu/P2000/tips/index.htm

Parent/Teacher/Student Conferences

The purpose of conferences is to communicate student learning progress to parents. The timing and frequency of parent/teacher conferences vary from school to school, but no matter when conferences happen in your school, there are certain things you need to do to prepare.

Getting Ready for Parent/Teacher Conferences

- Prepare a folder of the student's current work that includes:
  - Three examples of the student's best work.
  - Student's current progress report or grade report.
  - Follow-up or next steps form.
- Construct a realistic agenda and share it with parents. Agenda items may include:
  - Something personal and positive to share about each student.
  - Student work and progress report or grade report.
  - Next steps—learning goal for each student.
  - If students attend with parents, prepare an age-appropriate question to ask students about their learning and/or progress.
- Provide a take-away—that is, information parents might find useful regarding their children's education. Take-aways may be articles about parenting, family activities that connect to a new unit, lists of magazines or books for children, district resources available to parents and students, and other topics of interest to parents that connect to students' grade level content and age.
- Prepare activities for siblings while parents meet with you. This might include coloring sheets, word activities, or number activities.
- If conferences take place in classrooms, arrange a table and adult chairs where you and parents can sit side by side.
- Provide water.
- Dress professionally.

During the Parent/Teacher Conference

- Introduce yourself to the parents, using your first and last name. Address parents as Mr., Mrs., or Ms., unless otherwise directed. Make sure you know last names, which may or may not be the same as the student.
- Use a conversational communication style and avoid educational jargon. If you are discussing a new instructional strategy, define it or have information about the strategy available, possibly in a take-away.
- Listen carefully and observe nonverbal communication.

Challenging Parent/Teacher Conferences

Sometimes parents become angry with their child or with you. Preparing for those infrequent moments will pay off. When a parent gets angry at you and/or uses inappropriate or abusive language, take the following approach:

- Remain calm, write down what is being said, and stay silent until the parent stops talking. Do not become defensive or argumentative.
- End the conference as politely as you can and suggest rescheduling the meeting. Use phrases like, "I understand you are upset; perhaps we should reschedule our meeting when everyone is calmer." "I think we should end the conference and reschedule it for another time." Stand up, walk out, and go to the main office.
- Write a short description of the conference and what was said. Share this with the principal or another administrator. If another conference is scheduled, request an administrator be present.

When a parent gets angry at a child and/or uses inappropriate or abusive language, try this approach:

- Ask the child to leave the room to allow you to talk to his or her parents.
- Gently ask the parent to calm down. Try to redirect the parent's attention to one or two goals related to the child's progress that may make the next conference or grade report more positive.
- If calming down the parent appears impossible, end the conference as politely as you can, suggesting rescheduling the conference. If you are concerned about the child, excuse yourself and call an administrator for assistance.
- Write a short description of the conference and what the parent said. Share this with the principal or another administrator. If another conference is scheduled, request an administrator be present.

Family Involvement In and Out of the Classroom

Master teachers extend learning beyond the classroom into the home when they plan learning activities for families. Learning activities should deliberately connect to classroom curriculum, providing students a variety of ways to apply knowledge and skills. The suggestions that follow may serve as a catalyst for planning unique family projects that extend the curriculum beyond the classroom walls. Family projects provide parents additional opportunities to be involved in their children's education while providing teachers with more information about their students' families. The more teachers know about their students, the better teachers can facilitate students' learning.

Family Class Book

A Family Class Book chronicles the heritage of each student's life and family. Every family contributes one to three pages that include drawings, photographs, and information about the student's family life. The Family Class Book can become part of the language arts curriculum since it involves reading and writing. More important, it is another way to build classroom community and directly involve parents. Here are some resources for creating Family Class Books.

- Check out *Read, Write Think:*
  http://www.readwritethink.org/lessons/lesson_view.asp?id=941.
  It includes excellent lesson plans for creating Family Class Books.
- Read the bilingual children's book, *Family Pictures/Cuadros de Familia* by Carmen Lomas Garza to the class. It is a model for creating a Family Class Book with further suggestions for classroom implementation.
- Invite parents to include information about family and extended family members including family history, interests and hobbies, favorite foods and recipes, traditions, and celebrations.
- Ask parents for help with organizing and binding the book.
- Allow each student to check out the original Family Class Book overnight and have the book prominently displayed in the classroom for visitors to read.
- Make a photocopy of the Family Class Book for each student.

Flat Stanley Project

The Flat Stanley Project is based on a book titled *Flat Stanley* (1992) by Jeff Brown. A Flat Stanley is a drawing of a school mascot, animal, or whatever students decide it should be. Students color an outline of the chosen Flat Stanley and then choose relatives and friends to whom they send Flat Stanley, accompanied by a letter explaining the project. The letter asks recipients to take pictures of Flat where they live, doing something they would do. For example, Flat Stanley might be photographed at the Empire State Building or playing a family basketball game. Flat Stanley is sent back with a letter describing his or her adventures. For more information about Dale Hubert, the creator of Flat Stanley, and how to implement a Flat Stanley Project, check out http://www.flatstanley.com or Google "Flat Stanley." This is a great way to teach geography, world cultures, diversity, and to learn more about students' extended families. (See the Flat Stanley example on the CD.)

The Teddy Bear Project

The Teddy Bear Project is another project that supports classroom community. Elementary classrooms around the world participate in a teddy bear exchange to foster tolerance and understanding of different cultures. Each class dresses a teddy bear (or any stuffed animal) and chooses a name for its bear. Classes around the world exchange teddy bears. They take pictures of the visiting bear taking part in classroom activities. Each class keeps a journal for the visiting bear. Pictures, letters, and emails are exchanged. As part of the project, the visiting bear spends an evening or a weekend with each student. The student and family complete a journal entry and include photos of the bear's visit. Eventually, the bear returns to his or her home classroom with a journal and picture album. Check out http://media.iearn.org/projects/teddy-bear for more ideas on how to implement the Teddy Bear Project.

Family Homework

Family homework provides real-life situations for students to apply concepts and skills they are learning at school. These assignments involve parents in their children's learning and are designed to be integrated into a family's weekly routine. Create a monthly calendar of family homework assignments that connect to current class curriculum. Send a letter to parents describing family work. Students and parents may choose from a menu of homework assignments. (See Family Homework

Letter, Family Homework Assignment Form, and Family Homework Sample Calendar on the CD.)

Example of Family Homework Letter

September 4, 2010

Mrs. Smith's Third Grade Classroom — The Eagles
Elmwood Elementary School

Dear Families:

We are off to a great start this year. Now we are ready to begin some important and interesting work.

Homework is an important aspect of your child's education. Good assignments help students practice and apply skills and concepts learned in the classroom. Family homework lets you see what your child is learning.

As part of our content curriculum, I will be assigning one homework activity each week for parents and students to complete together. You will have a menu of choices, and we will vary the content focus. In preparation, a calendar of homework choices will be sent home each month. These will also be posted on our class Web page. Family homework will be turned in each Monday. A new calendar will come home each month.

All Family homework is linked to our school curriculum and learning objectives. You are not asked to teach; just enjoy the collaboration of completing these activities with your child. Feel free to involve the entire family. Each Monday your child will turn in a completed Homework Form (attached) that will identify the assignment you completed and contain feedback from both you and your child.

Please contact me if you have any questions or concerns.

Sincerely,

Mrs. Smith

Math Activities
- Plan a food budget.
- Make a grocery list and go grocery shopping together.
- Clip coupons and calculate how much was saved by using them.
- Cook dinner together. Use measuring cups and spoons to measure ingredients.
- Calculate the cost of driving to the park instead of walking.
- Help your child open a savings account and meet each month for a budget conference.
- Invest in the stock market with play money.

Resource for Math Homework
- At Home with Math (for ages 5 to 11): http://athomewithmath.terc.edu/

Social Studies Activities
- Research your family tree and create a diagram to share with the class.
- Interview older friends and relatives and record the conversations as a living history project.
- Research the history of your neighborhood and local area.
- Explore local opportunities for walking tours and special events.
- Instead of theme park vacations, explore your state. Make a plan to stop at historical markers. Create a photo journal.
- Visit and volunteer at your local historical society.
- Visit local ethnic fairs and festivals.
- Visit a local farm.
- Visit a farmers' market.
- Keep a map in the car and have your child give you driving directions.
- Practice map skills and plan driving routes for short and long trips.
- Check out Geocaching: http://www.geocaching.com/
- Check out Letterboxing: http://www.letterboxing.org/
- Visit city hall or a court house.
- Attend a school board or city council meeting.
- Visit your state capital. Make an appointment to meet your state representatives.

Science Activities

- Make a plan to recycle at home.
- Visit local museums.
  - Check the Web site for educational activities.
  - Many offer family activities.
- Visit the zoo.
  - Check the Web site for activities.
  - Most offer family activities.
  - Find out what benefits are available for zoo membership.
- Visit a local nature center.
- Do at-home science activities for children and families: http://www.tryscience.org/parents/se_1.html
- Experiment with growing crystals: http://rockhoundingar.com/pebblepups/growcryst.html
- Make playdough: http://www.teachnet.com/lesson/art/playdough061699.html
- Make oobleck: http://www.science-house.org/CO2/activities/polymer/oobleck.html

Literacy—Reading Activities

- Visit the local library. What programs are available for students and families?
- Have a regular family reading time—DEAR—Drop Everything And Read. Everyone reads a book.
- Talk about what you read. Retell. Sequence. Plot. Perspective. Characters.
- Read the newspaper together.
- Read recipes together while cooking.
- Provide a wide variety of reading materials, such as newspapers, comics, magazines, books, picture books, story books, graphic novels, and manuals.
- Read labels and directions together.
- Read a book and then see the play or movie based on the book.
- Choose a read-aloud book or a book on tape/CD for a vacation or weekend trip.
- Choose a series of books to read aloud every night before bedtime.

> **What Experts Say:** Writing profiles of family or community members encourages students to discover their passions through questioning, exploration, and discovery. (National Middle School Association, 2003)

Literacy—Writing Activities

- Write a description of something you ate this week without mentioning the actual food. After writing it, give the description to someone to guess the food.
- Write descriptive clues for a treasure hunt game with your friends.
- Conduct an interview and publish it.
- Write to a pen pal or email pal (with parent permission).
- Write a movie review.
- Write a book review.
- Add pizzazz to a parent's shopping list by using descriptive adjectives and adverbs before each item, such as perfectly precious plums.
- Send a note to a special person, such as a teacher, principal, grandmother, grandfather, aunt, uncle, or cousin.
- Draw a picture and then write a description of it.
- Make a Vacation Photo Essay Scrapbook. (You can do this on the computer if you have a digital camera.)
- Take pictures of a special event, such as a baseball game or party. Sequence the pictures. Then write a short story or comic strip with a beginning, middle, and end.
- Write a "How-To" for something you enjoy doing.
- Write a "To-Do" list for your parents.
- Write a friendly letter to a family member who lives out of state or out of the country. Ask for maps and tourist guides to learn about the place.
- Write yourself a letter. Date it and ask someone to send it to you in five or more years.
- Write yourself a letter outlining goals you would like to set for yourself in the coming school year. Ask someone, such as a parent or teacher, to give you the letter at the end of the year.
- Write a persuasive letter to your mom or dad, convincing him or her to give you something you really want.

- Send yourself a postcard from places you visit over break. Describe everything using adjectives, verbs, and adverbs. Collect them and put them in a memory book about your trip.
- Create a brochure about a special place you visited, urging people to visit that place.
- Think of a place that you visited or a special event that happened to you. Write an advertisement that would make people want to visit your place or have an event like yours. Illustrate your writing.
- Keep a daily journal. Include pictures and write captions for them.
- Make a menu for a restaurant and describe the food in each entrée.
- Copy your favorite cookie recipe.
- Write ten questions you want to ask your teacher.
- Write an adventure for one of your favorite characters from a movie, book, or graphic novel.
- Publish a family newsletter. Include features about family members.
- Create a new idea for this list.

Arts Activities

- Visit an art museum, art gallery, or art show.
- Complete a craft together. (Google "arts and crafts" for unlimited ideas.)
- Go to a children's theater production.
- Go to a concert. (Many local concerts are free.)
- Make a musical instrument.
- If you play a musical instrument, teach your child how to play it.

Chapter 4
Engaging in School Culture

When teachers develop allies, they remain fresh, committed, and hopeful.

—Sonia Nieto, Professor Emeritus of Language, Literacy and Culture
University of Massachusetts, Amherst

Mary, First Grade Teacher

By Thanksgiving, I learned that nothing gets ordered or approved without the consent of the building secretary. She is the person who orders materials, assigns rooms, approves purchases, communicates information, and provides or denies access to the principal. Getting to know her work habits, her communication style, and her love for chocolate have really served me well. I'm already beginning to feel part of the building community. I've made friends with a reading specialist, my grade level team, and the custodian—he likes the Green Bay Packers. Rushing out of the building at the end of the day robbed some of my colleagues, who were hired at the same time, the treasures I have discovered in the time I have taken to build relationships.

I've learned that there are so many people in the building who can help me do my job better. For example, I stopped down to visit with the school counselor the other day because I was concerned about one of my first graders. He seemed uncomfortable playing with the other children during recess. After describing his behavior, the guidance counselor shared some ideas about it and offered to invite the student to a student friendship group. She was a wealth of information.

Introduction

Mary has learned that working with others in her building gives her information, resources, and ideas that enable her to become an integral part of the school culture. She understands there is a protocol for acquiring necessary classroom materials, reserving space in the building, or referring students for special services. Ultimately, she knows that by forming relationships with other faculty and school personnel, she can better serve her students' needs while also promoting a positive working culture among the adults in the building. Mary is lucky. These skills come naturally to her.

Healthy connections among staff and faculty in the building serve as a model for students and their families. Often, dysfunctional school cultures can trace the root of the problem to poor communication practices, the inability to work together, or the isolation of staff and faculty. Building a community takes an intentional effort. By reaching out to others and getting to know people, teachers build relationships. It is only through positive relationships that people trust each other and invest themselves in the community.

> **What Experts Say:** The nature of relationships among the adults within a school has a greater influence on the character and quality of that school and on student accomplishment than anything else. (Barth, 2006)

Tools and Strategies for Building Relationships with School Personnel and Faculty

Leadership Personnel

All schools have leadership personnel that include principals, assistant principals, and lead teachers. All districts have leadership personnel that include superintendents, assistant superintendents, school board members, and union/uniserve directors. Although meetings with district personnel may be limited and building relationships more challenging, the following tools and strategies will help facilitate the process of meeting people at the district level.

- Introduce yourself to those in leadership in your school. Schedule appointments to initiate a professional relationship. Invite the leader to share ideas about the vision and mission of the school and how you might support both in your classroom.

- Invite the superintendent, assistant superintendent, and school board members to classroom events that showcase student work. Write thank you notes when the district has supported field trips, special class and school activities, and professional development activities.
- Attend events organized by the local union/uniserve and make it a point to introduce yourself to the director and elected teacher members.
- Attend school board meetings.

Support Personnel

Each school has a variety of support personnel including secretaries, custodians, bus drivers, security personnel, and food service staff. Secretaries and custodians are among support personnel with whom you probably have the most contact—make it positive.

- Make it a point to interact with support personnel, whether it's a smile and a nod or a short conversation. Listen and find connections that will become the basis for ongoing conversations. If you have already established a positive relationship with support staff, solving any problem that arises will be much easier.
- Turn in paperwork such as grades, forms, schedules, and anything the secretary has requested in a timely fashion. If you know something is going to be late, let the secretary know in advance.
- Communicate with the custodian when a class event might result in extra trash or the arrangement of classroom furniture might impede cleaning.
- Provide ample notice to food service staff when field trips or special class events include food and will decrease the number of students eating meals in the school.
- Get to know the bus drivers. What goes on in the bus impacts what goes on in the classroom.
- Meet the security personnel and/or police liaison and find out what you can do to make their jobs easier.
- Compliment! Look for things that are done well and/or were particularly helpful to students, parents, and teachers. Occasionally write an informal thank you note or a formal thank you that is copied to the leadership team.

Resource Personnel

Schools and districts have personnel that work with students, parents, teachers, administrators, and the community, such as social workers, psychologists, and health care professionals. Find out who these people are and how they can make a difference when a student requires more than what can be provided in the classroom. At a meeting, introduce yourself and invite the specialist to share the services he or she might provide or arrange. After the meeting, follow up with a summary of the plan, your involvement, and a thank you.

Resource Teachers

Resource teachers are treasures available to all classroom teachers. Library Media Specialists, Instructional Technology Specialists, Reading Specialists, Content Specialists, Special Education Specialists, English Language Learner Specialists, and Gifted and Talented Specialists may be assigned to individual schools or provide district-wide services. Introduce yourself to resource teachers early and establish what type of collaboration would benefit students. Invite them to help you plan instruction, model new strategies, or work with specific students. Occasionally write an informal thank you note or a formal thank you that is copied to the leadership team.

Para-Professionals, Instructional Assistants, and Other Education Support Personnel

Education Support Personnel (ESP) such as para-professionals and instructional assistants work with students and teachers for a wide variety of reasons. Establishing a working relationship with each person is paramount to establishing a positive classroom culture. Become familiar with the job responsibilities of each ESP and set up a meeting to discuss the best way to communicate and collaborate. Discuss classroom expectations and norms so there is a united front. Recognize and acknowledge ESPs' challenges and accomplishments on a weekly basis. Provide feedback and support. Occasionally write an informal thank you note or a formal thank you that is copied to the leadership team.

Other Teachers

Other teachers include grade level teachers; special education teachers; and music, art, physical education, world language, and technology teachers. Forming a relationship with all the teachers who work with your students benefits both you and your students. Establish how to work together so you can set schedules and prepare students and classrooms. Communicate how all teachers can reinforce knowledge and skills across the curriculum. Consider inviting special area teachers to be a part of the yearly unit planning. Occasionally write an informal thank you note or a formal thank you that is copied to the leadership team.

Building Relationships with Substitute Teachers

Organization and planning are critical for successfully supporting substitute teachers in the classroom. Keep a substitute folder in a safe but easily accessible location, and keep it current with specific lesson plans for at least one week in advance. This includes making sure materials are ready and handouts are copied. Circumstances may require an extended absence from the classroom; having at least a week's worth of lesson plans will facilitate the substitute teacher's work so no instruction time is lost. Prepare students for the possibility of a substitute early in the year and possible activities they may do with a sub. Give them responsibility for welcoming and supporting the sub. If you know you are going to be absent, tell your students. Preview the lessons with students and provide preliminary directions.

Substitute Teacher Folder (see checklist on CD)

- Welcome letter for substitute. (See CD for Substitute Letter.)
- The contact information for a teacher or administrator who can share confidential information regarding special needs students, students with behavior problems, or any other special circumstances.
- Emergency Lesson Plans: Stand-alone lessons a substitute can follow without directions from you. Make sure all materials are available.
- Student activities that can be used as fillers. Supply enough copies with directions for classroom activities or games. Include answer keys.
- Map of the building with labels or notes.
- Morning Routine: Explain all of the morning procedures, including attendance and lunch count procedures. If this is done on a computer, include specific directions and codes.
- Dismissal Routine: What do you do to get ready to go home? Give clear directions for bus riders, walkers, and students with per-

mission to go home with another student. Some older students may be buddies to kindergartners and will leave early. Be sure to explain these procedures.

- Copy of Classroom Norms
- Attention-getting signals used in the classroom.
- Daily Schedule: List of class activities, recess, lunch, and specials. Include a labeled school map with locations for specials classes and grade level exits for arrival, dismissal, and recess.
- Identify students who leave the room, when they leave and return, and where they are going. If possible, leave the phone or room number of the teacher or specialist with whom the student will be working so that the sub may call and confirm the routine. (See CD for Traveling Student Log.)
- Class list/seating chart with student pictures. (Keep it up to date.)
- Identify students who are responsible helpers.
- Identify students with allergies and emergency routines.
- Policy for snacks and food in the classroom.
- Bathroom and hallway procedures.
- Lunch room procedures for students and teachers.
- Discipline procedures.
- Where to find workbooks, teacher's guides, and supplies.
- Names of nearby teachers with their rooms labeled on a map.
- School phone numbers.
- Who to call in an emergency.
- Teacher extra duties before, during, or after school.
- Parent helper/ESP schedule: Explain the role of parents and/or ESP in the classroom. ESP and parent volunteers should not be expected to take over the substitute's duties. Remind the substitute to respect confidentiality and not discuss students or the classroom with parents.
- Instructions for tornado and fire drills.
- Directions to the teachers' lounge and restrooms.
- Change for the vending machines.
- A feedback form for the sub to leave information for you. (See CD for Substitute Feedback Form.)

Classroom Activities for Substitute Teachers (see checklist on CD)

- **Board Games**: Play board games in case of indoor recess or unstructured class time.
- **Read-Aloud Material and Activities**: Choose a read-aloud book that students will like. Create activities based on the read-aloud, such as word searches, crossword puzzles, graphic organizers, coloring pages, or writing prompts for journal writing. (See the Read-Aloud Lesson on the CD.)
- **Routine Class Games and Activities:** Leave a list of those games and activities for the substitute. Tell students this is something they can teach the sub if you are ever absent. Be sure to leave directions for the sub.
- **Computer Activities**: Designate two to three technology student experts who can assist both other students and the substitute. Leave clear directions for using the computer lab. What are the procedures and expectations for student behavior? Leave login information and specific software and Web sites students may use. Suggested computer activities include math practice software and Web sites, keyboarding practice, Web quests connected to current instruction, and interactive Web sites.
- **Movies:** In case the substitute can't find materials or doesn't understand the lesson, leave an appropriate educational video or DVD of a movie that will engage students. Leave follow-up activities to go with it. (See Video Activity 1 and Video Activity 2 on the CD.)
- **Silent Reading:** Silent reading can give everyone a break and time to compose. Make sure you have a classroom library with books for students' interests and abilities. From the beginning of the year, make sure students know the procedures for selecting books and for DEAR (Drop Everything And Read). Leave directions for the substitute.
- **Enrichment Activities**: Have enrichment worksheets for extra practice, word searches, crossword puzzles, coloring pages, Mad Libs, cloze activities, and brain teasers.

Substitutes Who Miss the Mark

Substitutes who miss the mark may not have followed directions, did not get along with the students, and/or were unsuccessful at promoting the educational goals for the day. When possible, request substitutes you or other teachers know will work well with students. Review the preparation procedures for substitute teachers. Did you do everything possible to prepare and support a substitute teacher in your classroom? If you return to a bad report from a sub, talk to your students about classroom expectations, then let it go. Unless there were serious incidents in the classroom, do not punish students for behavior you did not witness. You have little control over what takes place in your absence. If you feel the substitute was a detriment to students, notify the principal.

Maintaining Relationships

Once initial relationships are established, maintaining relationships requires attention. Relationships go beyond the school community.

- Celebrate personal and professional achievements and milestones of all staff members, such as:
  - Wedding showers
  - Baby showers
  - Graduations
  - Anniversaries—both wedding and work
  - Retirements
- Birthdays
  - Locate a staff birthday calendar and put a small note or card in staff members' mailboxes on their birthdays.
  - Plan a monthly birthday lunch or breakfast.
  - If there is no birthday calendar, work with the building secretary to begin this tradition.
- Notes of appreciation for help or support or "just because"
- Notes and cards of sympathy or concern when colleagues experience a loss or encounter a difficult situation
- Attend visitations or funerals
- Family emergencies:
  - Provide meals. Cook meals or provide gift cards for prepared food.
  - Cleaning service. Collect money for a gift certificate for a cleaning service.

- Organize family support that may include babysitting, transportation, and hospital visits.
• Plan informal gatherings for faculty and staff to get together and connect, including:
  - Potluck lunches on teacher work days or Fridays
  - Coffee and treat days before school
  - Friday get-togethers: Meet at a local restaurant to share, celebrate, and de-stress.
• Secret Pals. Everyone likes to get a treat. Organize a secret pal program. It doesn't have to be connected to a holiday.

What Experts Say: In short, the relationships among the educators in a school define all relationships within that school's culture. Teachers and administrators demonstrate all too well a capacity to either enrich or diminish one another's lives and thereby enrich or diminish their schools. (Barth, 2006)

What Experts Say: Improved student achievement can be seen when teachers make changes in their practice by engaging collaboratively with their peers in a learning-team model. (Chappuis, Chappuis, & Stiggins, 2009)

Challenges to Building Relationships: What to Do When They Won't Talk to You

Any school will have a variety of personalities and differing levels of experience and professional practice. Do not let the lack of professionalism on the part of others affect your practice. It is your responsibility as a teacher to maintain a professional demeanor at all times. Even when colleagues choose to avoid you, treat them with professional courtesy. Continue to smile and acknowledge all colleagues. Avoid sarcasm when colleagues have differing ideas and opinions. Keep controversial issues professional, not personal.

Resources

Tips and Resources for Substitute Teachers (Education World): http://www.educationworld.com/a_curr/curr359.shtml

Lesson Plan Ideas and Teacher Resources (Thinkfinity): http://thinkfinity.org

Chapter 5
It's About Time

Time is the scarcest resource, and unless it is managed, nothing else can be managed.

—Peter F. Drucker, Father of Modern Management, Director of Drucker Institute

Kirstin, First Grade Teacher

About halfway through my first year of teaching, I came to grips with the fact that time was an issue. There just didn't seem to be enough of it. It is my nature to want to do the best I can and improve my professional practice. But I felt that some tasks were not getting accomplished. Things like a class newsletter, enrichment activities for my science units, and the book-in-a-bag take-home projects were things I'd like to do, but I found myself bogged down completing paperwork and administrative tasks with little time left for anything else.

During my second year of teaching, my personal goal and mission were to figure out what tasks could be systematized and what routines I could put in place to make tasks more manageable. What I discovered was that calendars, checklists, and storage bins were my friends. Calendars are easy tools to create and have helped me prioritize what needs to be done. I have collected bins, boxes, and shelving to get and stay organized. This year, I asked for a label maker for my birthday—what a nerd! Being organized means having more time for my classroom and me.

Introduction

Kirstin is like most new teachers. She is overwhelmed by all the responsibilities of being a teacher. For master teachers, organizational skills are a must. Fundamentally, organization is a result of choices made on a minute-by-minute basis. A balance must be struck between over-organizing—in which everything has to be done a certain way—and under-organizing—in which everything is delegated to later. Finding an organizational style that works for you is the key. Figuring out what makes you feel successful regarding organization is a good place to start. This chapter is about time—how to find more time, how to use it effectively, and how to manage teaching so it does not manage you.

> **What Experts Say:** "Time often defines the possibilities and limitations for teachers' professional performance." (Bacon, 1994, p. 12)

Calendars

Calendars can be managed in a myriad of ways. Paper calendars come in a day-at-a-glance, a week-at-a-glance, or a month-at-a-glance formats. Most teachers find a week or month-at-a-glance more useful because they provide more writing space, and school life revolves around the week as the primary unit of time. Another system to consider is a "day planner" that includes an address book in which to record student/parent contact information. Day planners also include space to maintain a communication log and to make to-do lists. Many teachers use electronic systems for calendars, address books, communication logs, and lists.

In addition to your personal calendar, establish a class calendar you can supersize to display in the classroom. Since so many families use the refrigerator door for display, create a cardboard replica of a refrigerator door where the class calendar is posted along with other important notices for the month. Your monthly class calendar should include dates for assemblies, field trips, grading quarters, progress reports, due dates for signed forms, monthly activities, take-home folder days, birthdays, fun events—anything that is connected to the classroom that has a date. A copy of the class calendar should be included in the class newsletter and posted on the class Web site. (See the Family Calendar on the CD.)

Construct a family calendar similar to the class calendar to post on your own refrigerator door. At the beginning of each month, write down work schedules, doctor and dentist appointments, school events, field trips, holidays, no-school days, sports practice, games, recitals, birthdays, parties, meetings, gifts and cards to have ready, social events, lessons, classes, and any other family or personal commitments. Consider displaying school lunch menus, school notices, permission slips to sign, monthly bulletins, an add-to grocery shopping list, reminders, chore lists, and important phone numbers, such as the substitute center and the attendance office. Having all this information in a central location will save you time every month. If you prefer to use a computer for scheduling, Google has a great (free) calendar feature that is easy to learn and fun to use. It also allows you to share your calendar with others.

Use Your Calendar Effectively

Establishing a calendar system is one thing; using it effectively is another. Create one master calendar with everything in it that you need professionally and personally. Carry that calendar with you at all times. Use it to construct the class calendar and/or a family calendar. Following are suggestions for using calendar systems more effectively to save more time.

- **Avoid overbooking:** When recording appointments and meetings, estimate the time required for each activity and note that on the calendar.
- **Contact information:** When recording appointments or meetings, include the name and contact information (phone number or email address) of the person involved. If you have to cancel or need additional information, there is no need to hunt for contact information—it's right there.
- **Weekly plan:** List the tasks for the week and the actions needed to accomplish them. Prioritize tasks. Determine what needs to be initiated and what needs to be completed during the week. (See the Task List template on the CD.)
- **New projects:** Use these steps to schedule time for new projects. First, visualize the whole project. Next, break it down into steps. Then, break those steps down into tasks. Finally, schedule time for each task.
- **Reality check:** Schedule the time you think you need to complete a task. Keep track of the time it actually took to complete, and compare it to the time that was scheduled. Make adjustments in the future. Maintain a weekly log that documents how you spend

your time. Pinpoint things that nibble away at your time and energy and prevent you from concentrating on more significant obligations.

- **Scribble Pads:** In addition to a calendar, carry a scribble pad for jotting down information and miscellaneous material that includes ideas, notes, inspirations, quotes, lists, gift ideas, book titles, authors or speakers, and new restaurants. Date each page or entry. Scribble pads provide easy access to information that often gets lost in the cracks.

Task Lists

Lists are the oldest and most basic graphic organizer. There are three types of lists: *basic, ordered,* and *prioritized.* A *basic list* is simply a compilation of items and/or tasks to remember to do. This could be a grocery list, a reminder of appointments, or a list of items to be photocopied for a specific lesson.

Ordered lists sequence the often routine tasks that need to be completed within a time frame. This type of list might include everything that needs to be done at the end of the day, such as close window shades, turn off the computer, and lock cabinet doors. Another example is a check-off list for students to help them organize their take home folders, (See the Take-Home Folder Check-Off List on the CD.)

Prioritized lists rank items or tasks based on importance and time. Lesson plans, for example, are prioritized lists that include what must happen first, second, and third in order for students to learn.

Master teachers use *task lists* that include all types of listings. Maintaining a weekly task list facilitates organization and saves time. A task list is a companion to a calendar in that it dictates what is recorded in a calendar and helps teachers manage personal and professional time. A task list describes what needs to be done and the estimated time to complete those tasks. Schedule time for constructing a task list. Create a template for a task list (see the Task List template on the CD), based on personal and professional demands and responsibilities. Items to consider in a task list are:

- **Immediate Action:** Tasks with deadlines and estimated time for completion.
- **Finish by End of Week:** Tasks with a weekly deadline and estimated time for completion.

- **Future Projects:** New projects to be completed in the near future but require scheduled time and a break-down of tasks. Estimate time for this task.
- **People to Contact:** Who, what, and when to contact and estimated time scheduled to make the contacts. (Include the "just because" positive parent phone calls. See Chapter 2.)
- **Meetings and Appointments:** Set up meetings or appointments or reconfirm dates, times, and/or place for meetings and appointments. Estimate time for this task.
- **Routine Tasks:** Schedule time for those tasks that need completion every week, such as grocery shopping, laundry, paying bills, and cleaning. Estimate time for these tasks.
- **Routine Paperwork:** Schedule time for grading student work and completing school-related paperwork. Estimate time for these tasks.
- **On-Hold Non-Urgent Items:** These include "would be nice, but not necessary now" items.
- **Professional Learning:** Schedule time for professional reading, attending workshops, or meeting with other teachers.
- **Relaxation and Fun Activities:** Schedule time personal time. Make this a priority.

Evaluate, React, and Move On!

Review your task list at the end of the week and determine if this week's planning worked for you. Continue with what worked and react to what did not. Here are some guidelines to consider:

- Don't waste your time on guilt about what you didn't get done.
- Don't allow frustration with uncompleted tasks to overwhelm you.
- Don't expect to get every task completed on the weekly task list. Life happens, and sometimes things do not get done.
- Review the task list throughout the day.
- Check off each task as completed and congratulate yourself.
- Check the following day's task list before leaving school and shift unfinished tasks to the next day or two as necessary.

Accept the reality that you cannot always expect to cross off all the tasks at the end of the week. If you are always left with a long list of unfinished tasks, do a reality check on yourself and your use of time. Enjoy what you do well and reflect on what you can do better.

> **What Experts Say:** "When teachers feel overwhelmed by the innumerous tasks of teaching, they can become less intrigued with learning new practices and lose their creative thinking abilities." (Collinson & Cook, 2000, p. 6)

Going Green in the Classroom

Even in light of current technology, paper piles up. Going green in the classroom saves trees and models global citizenship. If paper piles abound, here are some ways to attack them and strategies for preventing the pile up. First, paper piles need to be deconstructed. Implement RSVP: Read, Store, Vote, Purge.

- **Read**: Create a reading folder, notebook, or box. Tear out the articles you want to read and recycle the rest of the journal or magazine.
- **Store:** These are papers that must be kept for reference later. Take the time to immediately file them in a filing cabinet, file box, or another site designated for important papers.
- **Vote:** Select papers that require your immediate attention. However, wait until you finish sorting before acting.
- **Purge**: Be ruthless and toss anything you have not looked at for six months. Don't keep extra copies. Ask yourself, "Do I really need this paper?"

Schedule time to RSVP. Designate a specific amount of time for sorting and responding each week.

Avoid New Paper Piles

Once you have eliminated the paper piles, avoid new piles from forming by following these suggestions:

- Clear off your desk every day. When you return to it in the morning, you won't spend time rearranging things and putting away files or piling papers on top of what is already there.
- Establish an in-box and clear it out every day, sorting its contents into RSVP.
- Make it a goal to handle each paper only once. Try placing a red dot on each piece of paper every time you handle it. When the paper looks like it has the measles, ask yourself. "What do I need to do to get this job done?"
- Return phone calls, respond to email, and deal with parent communication as received. Check voice mail and email twice per day.
- Schedule time daily to address student work.

> **What Experts Say:** Feedback needs to come while students are still mindful of the learning target and while there is still time for them to act on it. (Brookhart, 2008)

- If you discover you're tossing the same things each week, consider stopping subscriptions to magazines you are not reading and getting off junk mail lists. If you want to be taken off as many national mailing lists as possible, the first step is to contact the Direct Marketing Association's (DMA) Mail Preference Service. Register with DMA at:
  https://www.dmachoice.org/dma/member/regist.action.

The Number Filing System

The number filing system does not depend on filing items alphabetically by the first letter of the first important word on the name of a file. Each file drawer is assigned a number. The first file starts with the number of the file drawer plus a number for the file. For example, if you decide that the first file drawer in a file cabinet is 1,000, then your first file is 1,001. The first file is the master file that contains a list of each file's number and contents as follows:

File #	File Contents
1001	Master list
1002	Book inventories that include each student's name and book # assigned
1003	Strategies for modifying assignments for LD students
1004	Evaluations from principal for 2009 and 2010

The advantage to this system is that you can look in the first file at the master list and find the number of the file along with a description of its contents. Each file simply contains a number on the tab. Each file drawer receives a different number. For example, the second drawer might be the 2,000 series, and all files in that file drawer would start with 2,001, 2,002, etc. Files can just continue to be numeric without grouping them by subject matter or content, which makes it very easy to maintain and add to this filing system. Returning files is easier because you do not have to read cryptic titles and decide where the file should be placed.

Organizing the Desk

Organization of a classroom extends to your desk. Here are some organizational tips for your desk.

- **Desk Top:** Do not store things on top of the desk. Keep work areas clear of everything except for things used every day.
- **Desk Drawers:** Determine which drawers should contain items for quick accessibility (those supplies and items you use on a regular basis).
- **Supplies:** Store only those supplies you use on a regular basis in the desk. Store those items you use periodically in clear plastic boxes that are labeled and stored in another area.
- **Resources:** Keep calendar, district phone directory, reference books, resource books, and textbooks in one area of the desk.
- **Knickknacks:** Limit the number of knickknacks to only one or two items.
- **Classroom Office:** Create an office area in your classroom for your desk and file cabinets where you can work with minimum distraction.
- **Keys, Lesson Plans, and Grading Records:** Establish a specific place for school keys, lesson plans, and grading records that will

help someone else find them if you are not available. If you don't keep your school keys with you, place them in a desk drawer.

- **Litter:** Reserve one drawer for litter—that is, the miscellany that seems to have no special home when it appears on your desk. Empty the litter drawer completely once a month. Find a home for items that need one and discard the rest.
- **Emergency Kit:** Keep an emergency kit in a desk drawer that contains bandages, a sewing kit, cough drops, headache medicine, a couple of dollars, and breath mints. If you're a woman, add feminine products, an extra pair of nylons, and make-up necessities.
- **Blood-Borne Pathogen Kit:** Place this assigned kit in an easily accessible desk drawer.

Storage Strategies

No classroom ever has enough storage. Master teachers create storage for all the materials connected to units, bulletin boards, classroom activities, school activities, and resources. Following are tools for creative storage:

- **Plastic Storage Units:** These come in all sizes and colors. Like-sized storage units are stackable. Label all storage units. Clear plastic boxes help identify the contents quickly.
- **Plastic Zipper Bags:** These are great for storing markers, erasers, flash cards, game pieces, math manipulatives, and other small items. Gallon-size zipper bags are great for books or magazines that go home with the student. For units, three-hole punch plastic bags then place them in a binder with plans and other items related to the unit.
- **Copier Paper Boxes:** Copier paper box tops help organize materials for a learning center. The entire box is great for storing monthly bulletin board items. Cover these boxes in decorative paper or decoupage them in styles that match the contents. These boxes can be stacked on locker tops and cabinet tops. Cover stacked boxes with a vinyl table cloth to create a work area or learning center.
- **Tubes:** Store bulletin board border trim by wrapping it around mailing tubes, paper towel rolls, or even toilet paper rolls. Secure with paper clips.

- **Moving Boxes:** Check with a local storage or moving company for large boxes that will hold large flat materials.
- **Plastic Garbage Cans:** Store rolled posters and maps in plastic garbage cans, but be sure to label the container. If the garbage can has a flat top, cover it with a table cloth to create a work area or learning center.
- **Follow Through:** Make a habit of returning items to their original storage container as soon as you are done with them. And, sort through those items, discarding any out-of-date or damaged items.

A Potpourri of Time-Saving Strategies

Following is a potpourri of time-saving strategies master teachers use:

- **Student numbers:** Assign each student a number. It can be any number, or it can be the number that precedes the student's name in the grade recording system. Papers can quickly be put into numerical order, and they are ready to record.
- **Labeling Papers:** Train students to label each paper in their notebook or that they hand in with their name or student number, date, and other pertinent information. This saves time in identifying papers that slip out of notebooks.
- **Color Code Classes/Content Areas:** Use colored folders, index cards, Post-its, pens, and handouts—one color per class or content area.
- **Clipboards:** Buy several sturdy clipboards to hold current lesson plans, student checklists including items they are turning in, future lesson plans, and current bulletins or notices. You can stand clipboards up on holders on a desk or file cabinet, hang them on hooks attached to a wall, or hang them on file cabinets with magnetic clips.
- **Photocopy Box:** Place items to be photocopied in a box or wire basket.
- **To-Be-Sent-Home Box:** Keep a box or wire basket by the door for items that need to go home with students. Assign a student each week to help you remember to check the box before class is dismissed.
- **Three-Ring Binders:** Each student should have a three-ring binder to keep all handouts, notes, and assignments in one place.

Binders kept in the classroom insure that the student always has his or her work in class. Students take out all the papers after each unit, quarter, or semester. These papers might be sent home, saved for parent/teacher conferences, or transferred to a file that is kept at home until the end of the school year.

- **Three-Hole Punch:** Invest in a three-hole punch so all papers get punched and placed in students' three-ring binders.
- **Take-Home Folders:** Help students stay organized by establishing a take-home folder. Either provide a pocket folder, or ask students to bring one as part of their supplies. Establish a day of the week for folders to go home—for example, the folder goes home on Thursday and returns Friday with parent signature. Avoid sending materials on Fridays; they often get lost over the weekend. Use parent volunteers to help organize and fill take-home folders. Include a Take-Home Folder Check-Off List. (See the CD for a sample list.)
- **Student Information Folders:** Create a student folder for each student, where referrals, notes home, observations, reading records, and test scores are filed. Store student folders in file cabinets out of sight of other students or parents.
- **Homework Calendar**: Post a calendar on which you write assignments for each day. Create a file for each day of the month and put assignments, handouts, and/or worksheets in it. When a student is absent, he or she just needs to check in the file of the day he or she missed.
- **Homework on Web site:** Post class assignments on the class Web site. Make sure students and parents know where to look for an assignment when a student is absent.
- **Individual Absentee Folder:** Create and place an absentee folder on the absent student's desk. Assign another student to put copies of any handouts and missed work in the folder. Give the absentee folder to a parent or sibling who stops by to pick up the absent student's work. Laminating the folder with a message on the front such as "Absent today! We missed you!" adds a personal touch. Consider including a While You Were Absent assignment sheet in the folder. (See the CD for an example.)
- **Locker Magnets for Homework:** Each student places a magnet on his or her locker and then clips homework assignments for the day. The teacher can tell at a glance who completed the homework and who hasn't.

- **Student Mailboxes:** Student mailboxes can either be cereal boxes, stacking desk trays, or cubbies. You can use the mailbox system to distribute notes, announcements, and handouts.
- **Hanging Files for Returning Homework**: Establish a hanging file for each student and return homework by placing it in the files. Direct students to pick up homework at the beginning or end of a period.
- **Documentation:** Carry one sheet of self-adhesive return address labels. Make observation notes about students and later stick that label in the students' folders.
- **Transparency Binders:** Place overheads in page savers to extend their life.
- **Lesson Plan Books**: Record all of the school year dates, such as holidays, in-service days, open houses, conferences, grading deadlines, report cards, and special school programs, in your lesson plan book at the beginning of the school year.
- **Workshop Folders:** Bring a folder to each workshop. Label it with the workshop title on the outside. Inside, draw two vertical lines on both sides of the inside folder, forming columns in which to take notes instead of using handouts, paper napkins, or slips of paper. Place all handouts inside the folder. Before filing the folder, discard any handouts that aren't useful to you, copy those that may be useful to others, and either file the folder or place the handouts in a three-ring binder for easy reference.
- **Small Rolling Suitcases/Crates**: Invest in a small suitcase or crate that has wheels and a pull handle to carry papers, books, and supplies between home and school.
- **Procedure Posters:** Create posters that show classroom procedures. For younger students, use drawings, symbols, or pictographs to indicate how you expect students to do things in the classroom.
- **Recurring Procedures**: Create procedures for dismissal, movement of papers, movement of students, opening of class, quieting class, and seeking help.
- **Classroom Areas:** Establish one area in the classroom convenient to students that contains a stapler, scratch paper, hole puncher, pens and pencils, and a supply of tissues. Train students to use this area as needed.

- **Material Banks:** Establish a shared bank of materials. Put student volunteers in charge of the bank to distribute materials and make sure items are returned at the end of the period or day. When requesting your list of supplies, ask for extra pencils, pens, paper, markers, and colored pencils for the bank.
- **Daily Agenda:** Display a daily agenda of whatever is needed for the day that includes the date, class activities, supplies, texts, page numbers, handouts, and special materials.
- **Key Words:** Use a few key words consistently so your students learn what is expected of them easily. For example, when students hear "one-inch voices," it's a key to talk quietly.
- **Transition Songs:** Play specific songs to indicate specific procedures. (See Chapter 6.)
- **Five-Minute Warning:** Leave five minutes at the end of the period or the day for students to dispose of trash, return materials properly, and gather their materials. You might use a song of the week to signal clean-up time.
- **Assignment Design:** Be consistent in the design of assignments. Determine the student information you want on the assignment and why you want it. The assignment should state clearly and simply what the students are to accomplish. Number the steps to the assignment. When appropriate, add the academic standard the assignment addresses.
- **Rubrics:** Construct rubrics for projects, products, and performances.
- **Checklists:** Construct checklists. These should match rubric criteria.
- **Graphics:** Add a small graphic in one of the corners of an assignment that will quickly identify it in addition to its content or title. For example, "Take out the study guide for Chapter five. It's the one with the apple in the lower right-hand corner." Graphics can help students whose first language is not English.
- **Fonts:** Choose interesting fonts.
- **Space:** Leave plenty of space for student responses and use boxes to indicate the size of the response expected.

Strategies for Forming Groups

Using unique ways to form groups facilitates group activities, adds fun, and saves time. Here are some grouping strategies.

- **Sticks:** Use colored craft sticks to form groups. For example, form a group of students who all have the same color stick or a group in which all students have a different color stick.
- **Paper:** Use colored index cards, paper shapes, colored paper, or white index cards with stamped images or colored symbols on them to form groups by similar or different colors, shapes, or symbols.
- **Codes:** Code activity sheets or worksheets with highlighted words, colored symbols, stickers, rubber-stamped images, or by a punch (multiple holes, stars, hearts, diamonds). Again, form groups with identical or different symbols.
- **Cards:** Remove the kings, queens, and jacks from a deck of cards. Use cards to form groups by identical numbers, different numbers, numbers that add up to even or odd numbers, or by suits.
- **Novelty:** Use novelty items to form groups. Invite students to choose an object, party favor, pick-up stick, domino, game piece, colored paper clip, or button. Then, form groups with identical or different objects. Establish a storage box filled with these items.
- **Colors:** If you are using colored items in a group, colors can indicate order of group presentations, the leader, the writer, or the reporter.

Resources

Google "going green in the classroom" for current resources.

Wachter, J., & Carhart, C. (2003). *Time Saving Tips for Teachers.* (2nd ed). Thousand Oaks, CA: Corwin Press.

Chapter 6
Space Strategies

A well-managed classroom doesn't just appear out of nowhere. It takes a good deal of effort to create—and the person who is most responsible for creating it is the teacher.

—**Robert Marzano, Education Researcher and Author**

Lisa, Second Grade Teacher

The classroom I was assigned to my first year of teaching was full to the rafters of stuff. Mostly, lots and lots of boxes—there were old brown boxes, shoe boxes, plastic boxes, moving boxes, copier paper boxes, and even a hat box. In addition to the boxes, there were decrepit desks, mismatched tables and chairs, shifting shelving, stained and patched carpeting, and even a rocking chair with one arm missing. It was challenging to configure a classroom that allowed for movement and numerous instructional approaches. The students and I were constantly bumping into each other or searching for things we needed that should have been readily accessible. It took me the entire school year to sort through every box, bin, file cabinet, milk crate, shelf, and desk to cull out the items worth keeping. The summer between my first and second year of teaching was devoted to planning my classroom space. Finally, my classroom was ready to accommodate all of my students' physical needs as well as support large group instruction and small group collaboration, and make space for learning. Boy, did my planning pay off!

Introduction

The classroom environment can support learning when arranged suitably. Lisa had a lot of sorting and deciding to do as she moved into her assigned classroom. Other teachers will start in nearly empty classrooms with few resources. The question for teachers becomes, how do I plan my classroom's physical space to encourage movement, to allow for a variety of instructional strategies, and to reflect what I value as a teacher? Master teachers use the classroom space to support their educational goals. They see the physical space as a component of teaching that can motivate and engage students, reduce behavioral problems, and heighten learning. The classroom space should allow for easy access to instructional materials and supplies, limit disruptions and encourage harmony, and provide space for teaching and learning. Frequent disruptions and wasted time are outcomes of a poorly arranged classroom.

> **What Experts Say:** "You will get better results if you arrange your room to permit orderly movement, few distractions, and efficient use of available space." (Emmer, Evertson, & Worsham, 2003, p. 2)

Space for Learning

Arrangement of a classroom's physical space may be more important than many realize. Thirty desks arranged in five rows facing the blackboard and the teacher's desk is a paradigm of the past. Master teachers use all of their classrooms' available space. Sometimes the desks are arranged in groups of four for cooperative learning and other times in a U-shaped configuration for large group discussions. Whatever the arrangement of desks, it should reflect the lesson's learning goals.

Desks are not the only classroom furniture to consider; include informal furniture for other types of learning. Use soft chairs, pillows, and thick carpet squares for students to take on different learning postures.

Consider your students. Will any of them need wider aisles or special access because of physical handicaps or disabilities? Which arrangement will encourage student interaction and collaboration? Which arrangement will provide optimum proximity between teacher and students? One way to plan the classroom's physical space is to draw the classroom and classroom furniture to scale. Use the scale drawings to manipulate a variety of arrangements.

Space Strategies

Online Designing Tools

If scale drawing is not your strength, try one of these online software programs. These tools allow you to easily view your classroom in a variety of arrangements.

- **Scholastic Class Set-Up Tool:**
  http://teacher.scholastic.com/tools/class_setup/

  Class Set-Up is a new, easy-to-use, virtual layout tool that helps you design customized and effective classrooms to promote learning. Use this tool to rearrange and set up mock classrooms and map out virtual seating charts.

- **Design a Classroom!**
  http://www.atschool.org/materials/classroom/buildaclass/

  Design your own classroom. This tool allows you to create an ideal floor plan and hardware setup for your classroom.

- **Classroom Architect:** http://classroom.4teachers.org/

  Use this floor-planning tool to design a plan for your classroom.

- **Into the Book:**
  http://reading.ecb.org/teacher/design_classroom.html

  Design your classroom for better instruction and more fun.

The furniture arrangement, the choice of color schemes, and the type of interior decoration affects students' connectivity with that classroom. The classroom environment unconsciously influences students' sense of well-being.

What Experts Say: "Along with the physical arrangement of the room, you should consider how the room is decorated. Again, the physical appearance of the room conveys a powerful message when students first enter. It is important to note that the emphasis in decorating the classroom should be on functionality." (Marzano, Marzano, & Pickering, 2003, p. 98)

Classrooms can be altered in five minutes. Arrange the classroom so students can easily move the desks. Create schematics of the desk arrangement for each learning activity—open space for presentation, games, physical movement, role-plays and simulations, whole class discussions, small group discussions, cooperative learning activities, test-taking, and other learning activities. Share the schematics with the students. Provide time for students to practice quickly and quietly rearranging the desks. Make it fun by timing the drill and setting record times for rearranging desks.

Classroom corners and nooks are ideal places for reading and writing, conferencing, learning and interest centers, and places for students to retreat. Be creative with these corners and nooks. Find rocking chairs, bamboo chairs, beach chairs, bean bags, carpet squares, large pillows, small couches, and umbrella chairs in a variety of shapes, sizes, and textures. Resale shops, rummage sales, garage sales, and eBay are great resources for this type of furniture.

Feng Shui in the Classroom

Feng Shui is a Chinese science and system of organization that reveals the best way to lay out a room to "balance the energies" of the space and assure the health of the people who live or work in it. Some teachers find Feng Shui useful as they plan and decorate their classroom because the principles result in positive effects on classroom climate and student behavior. Following are a variety of Web sites and books on Feng Shui and its use in the classroom.

Resources

Classroom Feng Shui: http://classroomfengshui.com/

Feng Shui in the Classroom:
http://www.tabithamiller.com/learning/index.htm

Heiss, R. (2004). *Feng Shui for the classroom: 101 easy-to-use ideas.* Chicago: Zephyr Press.

Heiss, R. (2002–2010). *Feng Shui for the classroom: Creating a focused learning environment.* Retrieved 2009 from the National Education Association Web site: http://www.nea.org/tools/30045.htm

Keller, D. (2004). *Feng Shui for the classroom.* Kansas City, MO: Andrews McMeel Publishing.

Products that Promote Learning

Become aware of alternative products and tools designed to promote learning for students with specific needs. Bean bag chairs appear in many classrooms, but they are not often seen as therapeutic tools. Nevertheless, bean bag chairs can be soothing for students with Autism, ADD/ADHD, and Sensory Integration Disorder (SID) as well as students with varying needs and individual learning styles. Consult the physical and/or occupational therapist in the district for easy-to-implement ideas for classroom use such as weighted vests, air pillows, plastic squeeze balls, large rubber bands, or other possibilities for specific student needs.

Research into students' classroom needs has resulted in the availability of interesting products. Stability balls, which may positively impact some students' learning, are good for posture, strengthening muscles, improving balance, and increasing attention in the classroom. Desks with adjustable heights let some students to work while standing, allowing them to burn off extra energy and maintain focus. Physical and/or occupational therapists are resources who will help you learn about products and tools that might facilitate some students' learning.

Sensing the Classroom

Students and visitors formulate a feeling about the teacher and the classroom as soon as they walk in the door and look around. Make the classroom inviting and comfortable. As soon as students or visitors step in the room, they should feel the warmth of the environment. Think of the five senses as you create the classroom environment. Enriching the sensory classroom environment is a bridge to enriching the curriculum with the use of intriguing materials that cultivate students' intellectual curiosity.

Smell the Roses

Smell is an often overlooked but critical part of first impressions. Make sure the classroom is clean to avoid lingering unpleasant smells. Master teachers wipe desks and hard surfaces with an antibacterial solution or commercial wipe after students leave each day. Use antibacterial wipes to clean the computer keyboard and mouse. If the cleaning staff does not use an odor remover, consider purchasing one of the many on the market and spray the room at the end of each day. Try making your own potpourri or purchase one of the various commercial room deodorizers, including low-voltage plug-in deodorizers. Choose a clean fresh smell that is not overpowering or objectionable.

Sound Advice

Classrooms can be, and at times, should be, noisy places. Master teachers recognize that some students learn best when accompanied by sound and others learn best in silence. The classroom teacher's job is to be aware of the dynamics of sound by reducing unnecessary noise and heightening sounds that stimulate. To eliminate distracting noise, use old tennis balls over the feet of chairs and desks to muffle the noise. To enrich the learning environment, play soft music in the classroom as you get ready for the day. Music may have a calming effect on you and your students. It will welcome students and become an expected part of their morning routine. Playing soft background music may increase attention, improve retention, and focus learning. Music is also effective for transitioning and mood setting. Choose from a variety of genres: classical, instrumental, movie themes, rock/pop, or even nature sounds. Use a 60- to 90-second clip of a meaningful song for routine movements around the classroom. The following song titles are ideas for music clips that are great for specific routines:

- "Happy Trails": Use for five-minute clean-up at end of lesson.
- "Mission Impossible": Use for students to move into collaborative groups.
- "Celebration": Use when it's time to celebrate or recognize student accomplishments.
- John Phillip Sousa marches: Use to move students quickly from one activity to another or from one place to another.

Other sounds that are pleasant in the classroom include wind chimes and small indoor water fountains.

What Experts Say: Using music in the classroom may be helpful in establishing a positive learning state, creating a desired atmosphere, building a sense of anticipation, energizing learning activities, focusing concentration, increasing attention, improving memory, releasing tension, enhancing imagination, providing inspiration and motivation, and accentuating theme-oriented units. (Brewer, 2009)

Space Strategies

A Welcoming Sight

While you have little control over the classroom's physical lighting, there are things you can do to soften harsh florescent glare. Strategically placed lamps can provide both illumination and add a degree of warmth and softness. Use reading lamps to create a special reading corner or quiet nook. Check out rummage sales or eBay for unique lamps, but make sure they are safe and in good working condition.

Make classroom walls visually attractive. Wallpaper makes great backing for bulletin boards and is very durable. It is easy to staple up; sometimes single rolls are available at a discount. Outdated picture calendars (on sale after the first of the year) are great for bulletin boards. Make mini-posters of quotes that are motivational or connect to your content area. Display mini-posters on closet or cabinet doors. Remember when decorating the classroom to leave some blank areas for those students who do not need visual stimulation but do need a place to rest their eyes.

Touch and Go

For some students, touch is a primary way of learning. Acquiring knowledge through tactile experiences can provide an additional venue for understanding information. Use of manipulatives in math and experiments in science can greatly enhance learning for students who learn best by doing rather than hearing. Finger painting, model making, creating posters and dioramas, and playing games are well-suited activities for the tactile learner. Master teachers use flash cards (for math, vocabulary, and concept building), engage students in role plays, take students on field trips, and build movement into each lesson so students can experience learning in a physical way. Tactile learners may need to touch objects to understand them, so project-based learning and assessment are important for them. Alternative seating arrangements also work well for the tactile learner who may prefer to stand, sit on the floor, or curl up with a book in order to focus and learn.

Tasteful Classroom

Taste can be a challenging sense in the classroom. But occasionally, consider providing appropriate snacks that connect to a specific learning activity or celebration. Food can be a pleasant association between you, your students, and the classroom. Some teachers become associated with specific treats they have in their classrooms.

Resources

Classroom Organizing Tips (Scholastic):
http://www2.scholastic.com/browse/article.jsp?id=3635

Jones, F. H., Jones, F., Jones, P., & Jones, J. L. (2007). *Tools for teaching: Discipline, instruction, motivation.* Santa Cruz, CA: Fredric H. Jones & Associates, Inc.

Sensory Processing Disorder Foundation:
http://www.spdfoundation.net/

Chapter 7
Building Relationships with Students

No significant learning occurs without a significant relationship of mutual respect.

—Dr. James Comer, Maurice Falk Professor of Child Psychiatry, Yale University School of Medicine Child Study Center

Terry, Fourth Grade Teacher

Don't smile until Thanksgiving—that is the advice I heard from many experienced teachers before I started my first year of teaching. Apparently, smiling meant that I would not be able to control my class. I was baffled by this because I was excited to meet my students and create a positive feeling in my class where they wanted to be and wanted to learn. I decided to smile and smile a lot. Getting to know each of my students has been the biggest joy of teaching. Each child has a wonderfulness about them, and discovering this has allowed me to tap into how my students learn best. I've used this knowledge to build lesson plans, unit plans, and class activities that have the best chance of promoting my students' academic, social, and emotional growth. The relationship I build with my students is how I teach them. Unless I really know my students, I can't really teach them.

Introduction

The students in Terry's classroom are lucky because she takes responsibility for creating a classroom community by getting to know her students. Master teachers understand that building relationships with students, discovering who students are as human beings, and creating a positive climate in the classroom can maximize the time spent learning. A student-centered learning environment encourages social interaction, active engagement, and student motivation. Classroom management is shifting away from punishments and rewards toward engagement and community. No longer are students expected to be silent, passive learners. Instead, they are engaged in purposeful talk and tasks that will continuously develop their individual abilities.

The master teacher is deliberate in establishing a functioning learning community by devoting time and energy to building relationships. The relationship between the teacher and the student is perhaps the most significant piece of the learning equation, followed closely by the relationship among students. Master teachers use activities on the first day of school that initiate this process and persist throughout the school year to continue to develop and maintain positive individual and group dynamics. While getting-to-know-you activities begin the process of forming positive relationships, team-builders continue that process and are used throughout the school year.

> **What Experts Say:** "One of the most promising aspects of the teacher-student relationship is that it is not a function of what teachers *feel*. Rather, it is a function of what teachers *do*." (Marzano, Gaddy, Foseid, Foseid, & Marzano, 2005, p. 56)

Getting to Know Students from Day One

Building relationships starts on the first day of the school year with the teacher greeting students at the classroom door. Some teachers shake hands with every student, while other teachers greet students with a high-five. Master teachers use getting-to-know-you activities to make students feel comfortable in their new environment while providing an opportunity for students to see each other as unique individuals. These activities can be fun and get students and their teacher talking, sharing, and listening to one another.

Master teachers use procedures to acclimate students to classroom routines. As students come into the classroom, they are directed to a morning procedure that is posted in a conspicuous place. The morning procedure outlines the tasks to be completed daily. It also provides time for the teacher to leisurely greet each student. Morning tasks should take 10 to 15 minutes. Following is an example of first morning tasks. (See First Morning Tasks on the CD.)

First Morning Tasks

- Find your desk. Your desk is labeled with your name.
- Put your school supplies in your desk.
- Put classroom supplies in the labeled bins in the back of the classroom.
- Hang your backpack on the hook that is labeled with your name.
- Sit down at your desk.
- Open and read the letter on your desk.
- After you read the letter, write down one word that shows how you are feeling.
- Talk quietly to your neighbor until everyone is seated.

Learning Students' Names

Master teachers recognize the importance of using the students' names on the first day of school. It is better to mistake a student's name or mispronounce it than to make no attempt at all. Names are hard to remember because the concept of a name is abstract. Learning students' names requires deliberate action and practice. Here are some tips that may facilitate the process:

- **Rehearsal:** Study the class list before you see the students and rehearse each name aloud.
- **Name Tents:** Use name tents during the first week of class. Have students choose a colored piece of construction paper and fold it in half to form a tent. Direct students to print their names on the tent in large block letters and list three to five things about themselves. Prompts might include a favorite sports team, song, book, TV show, movie, musical group, food (sandwich, ice cream flavor, pizza topping), hobby, toy, action figure, or comic strip. When the tents are completed, ask each student to introduce himself or herself and share one or more things on his or her name tent.

Eventually, name tents can be stapled to a bulletin board to create a collage of students' names and favorite things. (This is a great bulletin board for the Open House.)

- **Name Tags:** Using name tags is similar to using name tents. Give each student a name tag with an adhesive backing or one that fits in a holder that hangs around the student's neck or is pinned on the student's clothing. Prepare name tags in advance. Invite students to add stickers to them. Use only first names, which allow more space for the stickers. For kindergarteners, send home name tag necklaces so they can wear them on the first day of school. Include the student's name and your name on each tag.

- **Photo Seating Chart:** Construct a seating chart with a photo of each student; ask students to sit in the same place for at least the first week. Make a copy of this seating chart to place in the Substitute Folder.

- **Circle of Names**: Direct students to sit in a circle. Ask them to think of adjectives that describe themselves that start with the first letter of their name. Provide a word bank of adjectives for each letter of the alphabet. (This is a good way to build vocabulary, too!) Start by modeling. For example, if your name starts with an *L*, you could pick the word *lucky*. Have the first student share his or her first name and an adjective. For intermediate grades, ask each student to share his or her name and adjective and repeat the preceding students' names and adjectives.

- **First Names:** Focus only on first names during the first week.

- **Attendance:** As you take attendance during the first week of school, say each student's name deliberately and make eye contact with him or her. While you take attendance, try writing something specific about each student to help you remember the person's name. Create a roster with students' photos, leaving space to note information students share on the Photo Seating Chart.

- **Name Round-Up:** At the end of the first day, attempt to say every student's name. If you can't remember a student's name, ask that student for the first letter, second letter, etc., until you can remember the name. Invite other students to do the same thing.

- **Keep Trying:** Let your students know you are actively trying to remember their names and the correct pronunciation. If you can't remember a student's name or the correct pronunciation, just ask! Students will really appreciate your effort in remembering their names.

How Do Students Get to Know Me?

It is as important for your students to get to know you as it is for you to get to know them. Introducing yourself as early as possible on the first day of school is imperative. Be creative with your introduction. Focus on facets of your life that will engage students and make connections to their lives. Share things about your family, pets, hobbies, travels, favorite sports and teams, and what you do in your free time. Two activities for introducing yourself are included on the CD: the Introducing Yourself to Students PowerPoint Presentation and the Me in a Bag Activity and Parent Letter.

Create a PowerPoint presentation using a theme that is not only used throughout your introduction, but also introduces the classroom theme for the year. The Introducing Yourself to Students presentation on the CD uses the theme of baseball. Choose a theme that reflects your personality. You can generate themes from a variety of topics, such as transportation, urban or farm life, world travels, games, sports, shopping malls, or whatever else strikes your fancy.

The Me in a Bag Activity starts with a bag filled with four to five artifacts that are interesting and tell something important about you. Model the activity, which introduces you to your students and demonstrates an activity they will complete in the next few days. Find an interesting bag that tells something about your personality or interests. Use a gym bag if you are interested in sports or a brightly colored shopping bag if you love to shop. Artifacts can be photographs, travel trinkets, sports equipment or team clothing, toys, postcards, ticket stubs, or anything connected to a facet of your life. Pull out one artifact at a time and explain its significance to your life. Hand out a bag for each student to fill their own *Me Bags*. Create a schedule so that each student shares his or her *Me Bag* over the next week.

> **What Experts Say:** "Teacher language—what we say to students and how we say it—is one of the most powerful teaching tools. It permeates every aspect of learning." (Denton, 2008, p. 28)

How Do Students Get to Know Each Other?

Students need to get to know and build relationships with each other. Positive relationships among students cannot be assumed; they need cultivation. Master teachers know that building relationships facilitates learning—first the relationship, then the learning. Once teachers know their students and students know their teachers, the teaching and learning process becomes more efficient. Getting-to-know-you activities and team-builders are easy to implement and fun to do. Lesson plans for the first week of school should include a variety of getting-to-know you activities and team-builders. Often these activities are developed around content and provide early assessment of students' strengths and abilities.

Getting-to-know-you activities are variations on a theme—questions and prompts that elicit information about students in a variety of formats. Student Interviews (see the CD) get students talking to each other immediately, and the culminating collage activity provides mini-posters to display in the classroom on the first day of school. Sign the Brick Wall (see CD) can extend from an individual activity to creating a life-size brick wall. Alphabet Squares, Bingo, Game On, Student Search (see example below), Stand Like Me, Dragon, and Team Statistics (group and individual) are yet other ways for students to interact, find what they have in common, and start building relationships. (See these forms on the CD.)

Student Search

Find someone in the class that represents each of the boxes below. Have the person sign his or her name in the box.

Has brown eyes	Likes to eat spinach	Is wearing earrings	Has a cat	Walks to school
Plays an instrument	Has red hair	Likes to swim	Has been to the zoo this summer	Likes to eat pizza
Has a last name that starts with an S	Has five letters in his or her first name	Has one brother	Is wearing jeans	Likes to read
Has a beautiful singing voice	Is wearing running shoes	Eats hot lunch at school	Is wearing a blue shirt	Has more than one pet

From the resource CD of *From Surviving to Thriving*. The original purchaser has permission to reproduce this page for use in his or her classroom.
© 2010 Lorenz Educational Press, a division of The Lorenz Corporation. All rights reserved.

Literature that Works for the First Week of School

One way to begin content instruction and build community is to use read-alouds, regardless of students' age. All students benefit from read-alouds. Good literature engages students in reading and writing in a nonthreatening manner. Use literature to create fun activities that allow students to express themselves, share their anxieties, and get to know each other. There are many excellent choices available. Try *Chrysanthemum* by Kevin Henkes when you are learning new names, *The Kissing Hand* by Audrey Penn for kindergarten, or *The Fourth Grade Wizards* by Barthe DeClements. (See the CD for Literature for the First Days of School.) Check with your librarian, reading specialist, or other teachers to see what literature is available and what they have used.

How Do I Learn About Students' Interests, Likes and Dislikes, Families, Learning Styles, and Abilities?

Getting to know each student is one of the most interesting and challenging parts of teaching. First impressions are important, but digging deeper to discover students' learning style preferences, family dynamics, talents, work skills, study habits, interests, and background knowledge takes time to gather. Master teachers use this knowledge to plan appropriate instruction and assessment in order to help all students achieve success. Many tools and resources are available to discover information about individual students. Use simple interest and content inventories as a starting point. (See the Inventories for Reading, Writing, and Math on the CD.) Check with resource teachers to see what inventories your district uses. The Internet is also a rich resource for inventories.

How Do We Work Together?

Procedures are the daily routines of the classroom, and they begin on the first day. Master teachers clearly teach and model specific classroom routines and practices. Create step-by-step procedures that are ready to explain and model starting on day one. Predictable routines reduce students' and teacher's stress. Everyone knows what to do and how to do it. Master teachers trust students to make good decisions. Providing routines creates a framework that empowers students to take ownership of the classroom, themselves, and their learning.

Morning Routine

The morning routine includes what students should do without reminders every morning when they come into the classroom. Tasks might include unpacking, filing homework and folders, taking lunch count, collecting library books, processing notes from parents, collecting school forms, and beginning the morning activity.

Lining Up

Lining up is about moving from one place to another efficiently. Learning to line up in an orderly fashion is being a good neighbor to all the other classrooms. Master teachers have students line up in a certain order with a different weekly or daily line leader. This gives everyone a chance to be first but avoids the rush and scuffle for a place in line. Students may line up by class number or alphabetically. Have a hand signal for quiet and forward movement in the hallway. You do not want your directions to students to disturb other classes as you walk down the hallway.

Recess

Make sure students know what to do in preparation for recess, how to do it, and where to go. Assign two students the job of carrying the equipment bin to the playground and bringing it back with all the equipment inside at the end of recess. Let students know clearly when they may leave the classroom. Review behavior expectations for hallways and play areas. Clearly communicating expectations avoids unwanted recess situations. Occasionally go to recess with your students. It is a good way to see how students interact with each other and gives you opportunities to talk with students informally. Designate a signal for the end of recess. Explain where students should line up and again review the behavior expectations for the hallway.

Bathroom and Water

This is the time to talk about behavior expectations in the bathroom and the route between the bathroom and the classroom. This must be reviewed regularly to prevent problems. Many teachers have a laminated pass students may use when they need a drink or need to go to the bathroom. The pass is hanging in a prominent place. Students may take the pass and write their name on the board when they leave the classroom. If the pass is available, the student may take it, sign out, and leave. This is a good way to teach responsibility.

Specials—Coming and Going

Students leave the classroom throughout the day for music, art, and/or gym classes. Before your first special, discuss the behavior expectations outside your classroom when you are not there. The way students treat each other in your classroom should extend to other teachers' classrooms.

Computer Lab

Using the computer lab usually requires a journey down the hallway. It is important to have a routine so you do not waste valuable time. Assign computer seats before you leave the classroom. Most labs have numbered computers. Review and give students login information in the classroom and behavior expectations for the computer lab. Direct students to go to their assigned computers and login. Designate a couple of student experts to help students who have problems. Use established classroom signals for quiet in the computer lab. Consider a routine for student questions. Some teachers use green, yellow, and red plastic cups stacked on top of computer monitors. Green indicates everything is fine. Yellow indicates the student has a question but is willing to keep working and stay seated until someone can help. Red signals the student is stuck and needs help immediately but will stay seated until someone can help. Use your student experts to assist you.

Lunch—Coming and Going

Lunchtime requires a routine like everything else. Many schools have behavior expectations for the lunchroom that should be reviewed and practiced. Classes are assigned a time to go to the lunchroom. Plan a trip to the lunchroom during the morning of the first day of school to show students where everything is, where they should sit, and how they should behave. This is a good time to role-play going through the line and modeling appropriate behavior as they sit at the tables. Consider occasionally going to lunch with your students. You really get some good information from lunchroom conversations. Students usually go to recess from the lunchroom. Make sure they know where to go and which route they should take to get there. Review playground behavior and tell them where to line up to meet you at the end of recess.

Afternoon Routines

Establish a clear routine for the end of the day and begin it early enough to have quiet time together before the bell rings. No one wants to feel rushed and stressed as they leave school. Assign jobs for cleaning the classroom and putting everything in order. Afternoon tasks include assignment notebooks, take-home folders, and packing up. Plan a quiet activity for the end of each day. Consider having students reflect on the day by either writing in a journal, sharing with a partner, or sharing with the whole class about one thing they learned or liked about the day. Stand at the door and say goodbye to each student. Some teachers use that handshake, high five, or fist bump from the morning. This gives you an opportunity to talk to each child as he or she leaves.

During Instruction

Master teachers minimize disruptions during instruction by anticipating students' needs—from broken pencils to turning in assignments. Transition from one activity to another can result in loss of instructional time. Following are some suggestions for minimizing disruptions:

- **Classroom Signals:** Use a signal to get students' attention or get them to be quiet. Try hand signals like the "V" sign, thumbs up, or the "okay" sign; chimes; or a unique bicycle bell.
- **Pencils:** Many teachers have a cup of sharpened pencils ready to go. The student trades a broken pencil for a sharpened one. Sharpening pencils can become annoying when you are teaching. Make sure your students have a couple of pencils ready and you have pencils ready that they can borrow.
- **Paper:** Have a bin of paper available for students. It can be recycled paper from the copy room or odds and ends. Put paper and pencils on your wish list to parents in your newsletter.
- **Questions**: Create a procedure for students to ask questions during group work or when you are conferencing. For group work, consider having a small flag the group can raise indicating they need help when you can get to them. This encourages them to keep working and problem solving. If you are working with a student or small group, have a place on the board where student may sign up to talk to you when you finish.
- **Limiting Questions:** Encourage students to think and collaborate. Before asking you a question, students should ask three other classmates first. If no one has an answer, then they should ask you. For group work, include a Questioner as one of the group roles. Only the Questioner may access the teacher with a question.

- **Student Work Collection:** Establish a place for students to turn in work. Make sure students know what information should go on each assignment and where it should go.

> **What Experts Say:** "Proactively teach positive social skills: How to make friends, how to give compliments, what to do if someone teases you or hurts your feelings. Don't wait for negative things to happen." (Sapon-Shevin, 2008, p. 51)

Practice Routines

During the first week, teach and practice all routines each time you use them. It is not enough to just tell students what to do. You must teach and review routines in a variety of ways so all students learn them. Do this creatively and put the students in charge of teaching routines. Students can review routines by using role play and puppet shows. Following are some creative ways to teach and review routines:

- **Posters:** Students create posters to display in the classroom. Poster themes can include good study habits, friendly phrases, safety rules, and/or positive affirmations that promote the classroom culture.
- **Bingo, Bango, Bongo:** Create a bingo game that includes class expectations and norms.
- **Theatrical Performance:** Students create a play or mini-scenes that demonstrate the class routines and norms.
- **Wrong-Way Role Play:** Students create mini-scenes of poor behavior, and the rest of the class explains the problem and discusses solutions.
- **Road Signs:** As a class, select symbols that stand for a particular behavior expectation. Display road signs around the classroom.
- **Hey, Grandma:** Students write letters to grandparents or other relative, a neighbor, or a parent describing how they work with their classmates to assure a good working environment for everyone.
- **Brown Bag Moments:** Write the behavior expectation or norm on index cards and put the index cards in a brown paper bag. Every now and then, have a student pull a card from the bag and explain the behavior expectation or norm and why it is important.

- **Picture Rubrics:** Take pictures of students meeting behavior expectations or modeling a routine. Next, take pictures of students who are not meeting behavior expectations or are ignoring a routine. Use the pictures as guidelines. It's the process of doing it that makes the point.

How Can Students Take Responsibility for Their Classroom?

Assigning classroom jobs to each student builds student ownership. Students are capable of taking on the responsibility for doing those things in the classroom that benefit everyone. Following is a list of classroom jobs. Some are pertinent at any grade, while others may work better for younger or older students. Some teachers have students apply for specific classroom jobs. Questions on a Classroom Job Application Form can vary, based on the age of the students (see CD).

Student Jobs

- **Postmaster:** Puts all papers and/or announcements in student mailboxes
- **Caboose:** Last in line, shuts off the classroom lights and closes the door
- **Class Ambassador:** Greets visitors to the classroom
- **Calendar Assistant:** Assists teacher with the morning calendar
- **Messenger:** Delivers messages to other teachers or to the office
- **Line Leader:** Leads the class to destinations
- **Librarian:** Straightens up the bookshelves and returns books to the library
- **Census Taker:** Takes attendance
- **Lunch Clerk:** Takes the lunch count
- **Playground Equipment Manager:** Takes the bag of equipment out and in from the playground
- **Recycling Monitor:** Monitors the trash for items that should be recycled
- **Home Folder Supervisor:** Stuffs home folders and distributes them to students
- **Pledge Leader:** Leads the Pledge of Allegiance
- **Computer Cop:** Turns computers/monitors on in the morning and off at the end of the day

- **Math Tools Manager:** Distributes and collects math tools
- **Science Lab Assistant:** Distributes and collects science lab equipment
- **Techie:** Assists teacher and students as needed with technology

> **What Experts Say:** "In saying that a classroom or school is a 'community,' then, I mean that it is a place in which students feel cared about and are encouraged to care about each other. They experience a sense of being valued and respected; the children matter to one another and to the teacher." (Kohn, 2006, p.101)

How Do We Construct Norms Together?

Classroom norms are the behavior expectations for students and teachers. They are created by students with the teacher's guidance. Students who participate in forming norms are more likely to take ownership for their behavior, their participation, and their relationships within the classroom community. Master teachers have high expectations for student behavior and believe that students are inherently good human beings. Instead of dictating classroom rules, the master teacher provides the opportunity for students to identify and construct class norms that they value and have a stake in keeping. Through the building of class norms, students help establish a classroom culture that reflects who they are as individuals and as a group. A starting point to constructing norms might be the Classroom Bill of Rights lesson plan (see the CD).

Following are samples of possible class norms.

Our Class Norms
(Grades K-2 sample)
- Use kind words.
- Help each other.
- Take care of yourself, other people, and things.
- Be ready to learn.
- Be safe.

Our Class Norms
(Grades 3-4 sample)
- Respect yourself, others, and property.
- Cooperate with each other.
- We are all responsible for our community.
- Be prepared to learn

Bonus Materials on CD

- Baseball Theme and Activities
- Classroom Quilt Lesson Plan
- Crayon Box Lesson Plan with CrayonTemplate
- If You're Looking for . . .
- My Favorite Is!
- Questions to Prompt Critical Thinking

Resources

Kohn, A. (2006). *Beyond discipline: From compliance to community* (10th Anniversary Ed.). Alexandria, VA: Association for Supervision and Curriculum Development.

Alfie Kohn Web site: http://www.alfiekohn.org/index.html

Chapter 8
Responding to Student Behavior

I have come to a frightening conclusion. I am the decisive element in the classroom. It is my personal approach that will create the climate. It is my daily mood that makes the weather. As a teacher I possess tremendous power to make a student's life miserable or joyous. I can be a tool of torture or an instrument of inspiration. I can humiliate or humor, hurt or heal. In all situations it is my response that decides whether a crisis will be escalated or de-escalated, and a student humanized or de-humanized.

—**Hiam Ginott, Educator**

Peggy, Fourth Grade Teacher

Tony never seemed to have a pencil. It was the second week of school, and so far Tony had not been ready to start any work on time. His desk and locker were both messy disasters. I had gently reminded Tony to stay organized and keep his desk clean. I had also told him to please keep his pencils in his box and his notebooks ready. Tony promised faithfully every time that he would. He really meant it, but something just kept him from following through. Tony got along well with others, and no one seemed to mind that he was always last, even last in line. One day I walked with Tony on the playground, and we just talked. He had a great sense of humor and a natural curiosity. He was actively engaged in our class discussions and always did his work, though it was a little messy and a little late. Was it really such a problem that he could never find a pencil? Was I going to hound him about pencils and organization all year? I decided I could support

Tony without singling him out. I put a cup of sharpened pencils on my desk and told everyone in class to take a pencil when they needed one. Every Friday everyone would clean and organize their desks. I decided to work with Tony and gently support him without forcefully trying to change him. We had a great year. Sometimes I ran out of pencils. Some Fridays Tony would find ten of my pencils in his desk and return them to my cup. At the end of the year, Tony and his mother gave me a big box of pencils and a thank you note that said, "Thanks for helping me always find a pencil."

Introduction

Peggy has figured out that the way she acts, reacts, and models sets the tone in the classroom. Master teachers understand it is the decisions they make about students and procedures that will influence student behavior. They observe students to see what they do and why they do it, recognizing that all students have unique stories. They use this information to determine what course of action to take rather than making assumptions that what worked in the past will work with new students. Students are also observing the teacher. Especially during the first weeks of school, they look to the teacher to set the guidelines and boundaries they want and expect. The master teacher is in charge and must never abdicate the responsibilities of classroom leader.

Students will mimic what you model. If you are reasonable and flexible, students will know that you care about them. If you establish an environment that is safe and comfortable, students will trust you. If you show compassion to students, they will show compassion to each other. This chapter examines situations and challenges that occur in every classroom that require extra thought and careful planning.

Nonverbal Interventions

- A look—A frown or raised eyebrow
- A slight shake of the head
- Eye contact
- Hand signal
- Proximity—Stand next to the student.

Naughty Behavior

Naughty behavior consists of minor infringements of classroom norms or mischievous behavior. It should always be dealt with in the classroom and does not warrant

> **Positive Nonverbal Signs**
> - Smile
> - Nod
> - Eye Contact
> - Hand Signal
> - Proximity

responses beyond what the teacher and student can do in the classroom. It is usually corrected with a teacher look, a brief reminder, or student self-correction. Being present—that is, being aware of what is happening throughout the classroom—deters naughty behavior. Move around the classroom during instruction. Close proximity between you and students is a powerful tool in keeping them on task. Use nonverbal interventions when possible. A look, facial expression, eye contact, and a slight shake of the head or an established hand signal may be enough to stop naughty behavior before it escalates.

No matter how well lessons are planned, unwanted student behavior will still occur. Sometimes students become preoccupied with something to the degree that their attention is no longer on the lesson or activity. Other times students become bored or frustrated with the class activity because it is not challenging enough or it is too challenging. Like all of us, there will be times when students are in a bad mood or do not feel well. Along with different learning styles, students have different personalities. This variety of personalities means there will be times when they just don't get along. Also, students have a multitude of needs they bring into the classroom each day.

Be prepared to respond when the classroom norms are violated. However, always preserve the student's dignity. Never use sarcasm, ridicule, or embarrassment. Know your students and match a consequence to the misbehavior. One size doesn't fit all! Refer students to the classroom norms and gently remind students what is expected of them.

Sometimes students misbehave just to get attention from the teacher. Acknowledge the student and move on. For students who are struggling to change a behavior, be sure to notice good behavior. Let the student know you see when they are showing positive growth. A nonverbal response may be all it takes.

Challenging Behavior

Challenging behavior occurs when students lack strategies for controlling their own behavior. Be prepared ahead of time for challenging behavior. Think about the consequences that will support change in student behavior and not just punish them. Consequences are results or outcomes of behavior. They should make sense and be logical. When you assign a consequence, remain calm and quiet. If you are angry, wait until you can calmly speak to the student and explain why the behavior was unacceptable and/or counterproductive to the learning environment. We can dislike behavior, but we should not dislike our students. Let them know it is normal to make mistakes. As soon as possible, be sure to begin to rebuild a positive relationship with the student.

For students who are demonstrating unacceptable behavior, introduce them to a problem-solving process with which they can begin to take charge of their own behavior. Help them define unacceptable behavior as a problem that may have multiple solutions. Discuss different choices they could make to avoid or change unacceptable behavior. Over time, this will support students in their attempt to change and grow.

When a problem occurs, ask the student some simple questions. What did you do? Why did you do it? What were you feeling when you did it? What could you have done differently? What will you try next time? Provide a quiet place for students to go through this process before they meet with you for a conference to discuss their action plan for change. Students need time, practice, and support to become independent problem solvers. (See the CD for the Problem-Solving Plan Student Handout.) So, initially, work through the process with the student. Parent involvement may or may not be necessary at this point.

The Problem-Solving Process:

- Define the problem. What did I do?
- Analysis. Why did I do that? What was I feeling?
- Brainstorm. What are other choices I could have made? What could I have done differently? Think of at least three alternatives.
- Analyze the possibilities. What would have been the results of these actions?
- Select the best solution.
- Plan a course of action.
- What will I do next time?

Framework for Determining Interventions

Classroom Norms	Possible Interventions
Classroom norm is broken once	- **Warning:** Give the student a warning. - **Talk:** Have a talk with the student calmly and privately. - **Reflect:** Ask the student to think of a different action for the future. - **Apologize:** If the behavior negatively involved another student(s) or adult(s), ask the student to apologize for his or her actions.
Classroom norm is broken again	- **Warning:** Give the student a warning. - **Talk:** Talk about the behavior and not the student. - **Apologize:** If the behavior negatively involved another student(s) or adult(s), ask the student to apologize for his or her actions. - **Problem Solve:** Introduce a problem-solving approach to help the student plan strategies for changing future behavior. - **Monitor:** Monitor student progress.
Classroom norm is broken repeatedly	- **Think Tank:** Establish a quiet place in your classroom where students can go to calm down and think about the problem-solving process. - **Make a Plan:** Use a problem-solving approach for the student to examine his or her behavior and make a plan for change. - **Loss of Privilege:** Make sure the loss of privilege is a natural consequence and a last resort. - **Parent Contact:** Teacher phone call or note to parent. - **Student-Initiated Contact:** Student writes a note to parent describing his or her behavior and/or behavior plan. - **Parent Conference:** Formal conference with student and parents and any other pertinent school personnel.
Nothing works. Repeated attempts and approaches failed to support student change.	- **Referral:** Involve the school student support team that may be made up of administrators, counselors, special education teachers, social workers, psychologists, and/or other specialists.

> **What Experts Say:** There is a positive link between physical activity and the academic achievement of students. Students perform better on tests and were better able to pay attention after periods of physical activity, especially in reading comprehension. (Thompson, 2002)

Caution

Use detentions and loss of recess privileges sparingly. If you have a student who has trouble focusing or sitting still, loss of physical exercise and fresh air will only exacerbate the problem. If no other time is available, sometimes a detention or missed recess may be used as a problem-solving session. Use this time to talk and work with the student to clarify behavior, brainstorm solutions, and make a plan for change. This time together provides the teacher a chance to really talk with the student about the behavior and its causes.

Class Meetings

The purpose of class meetings is to provide a structure for students to address class behavior, problem solve, and plan activities like celebrations and field trips. The class meeting encourages group participation in creating classroom norms and procedures while building a sense of community and connectedness. Whether problem solving or planning, students have opportunities to practice life skills and the democratic process. It is a proactive approach to preventing problems in the classroom.

Start by setting an agenda for each class meeting. Agendas should be simple, specific, and take into consideration the appropriate amount of time for such a meeting for different grade levels. Here are suggested schedules and times for class meetings for various grade levels:

Grade Level	Schedule of Meetings	Length of Meetings
Kindergarten	Weekly—same time and place	10–15 minutes
Primary grades	Weekly—same time and place	15–20 minutes
Intermediate grades	Weekly—same time and place	20–30 minutes
Middle grades	Weekly—same time and place	20–30 minutes

Establish a structure for class meetings as follows:

- Check In: Students share a joy, give a compliment, or share something funny.
- Previous Issues: Provide updates on previous issues and actions.
- New Issues: Address new issues or upcoming events. Use a problem-solving process when appropriate for classroom behavior issues.
- Check Out: Brief summary of any action taken and responsibilities for the next meeting.

Examples of Class Meeting Agenda

Class Agenda 2nd Grade Wednesday 1:00–1:20 PM	Class Agenda 6th Grade Friday 2:30–3:00 PM
Check In: Share a compliment.	**Check In:** Share something that makes you laugh.
Update: Progress on field trip.	**Update:** Final plan on Science Fair.
New Issue: Pencil-sharpening crisis.	**New Issue:** RSVPs.
Check Out: Action taken.	**Check Out:** Last-minute details.

What Experts Say: "Students deserve to feel safe at school. But when they experience bullying, these types of effects can last long into their future: depression, low self-esteem, health problems, poor grades, and suicidal thoughts." (Olweus, 2009, para. #4)

Bullying Behavior

Bullying is any intentional action that inflicts physical or mental harm on another person. It is an act of verbal or physical aggression that may be both overt and covert and is repeated over time. Teachers should take proactive steps to identify bullying behaviors. Bullying behaviors include, but are not limited to:

- Spreading rumors
- Glaring or staring
- Telling lies
- Biting, pinching, scratching, pushing, shoving, kicking, pulling hair, tripping
- Sending nasty and/or intimidating notes on paper, through email, or texting
- Calling names or using mean or derogatory nicknames or labels
- Ignoring, shunning, and/or excluding someone
- Rallying others to dislike someone.
- Locking someone in a room, closet, or locker
- Taunting and making fun of others
- Using hurtful or mean language
- Extorting lunch money
- Rolling eyes and snickering
- Sexually harassing behaviors

Bullying is a problem of immense proportion that demands deliberate action. Know what your students are doing and saying. Listen in the hallways and on the playground. Observe with whom students choose to interact. Notice when students become quiet or withdrawn, act differently in the classroom, or miss several days of school. Determine the source of the problem. If the student's behavior is in response to bullying, plan for ways to intervene.

It is never acceptable to ignore bullying. It is not a normal part of childhood, and it rarely goes away on its own. Many incidents of school violence are directly related to bullying. It is up to teachers to stop bullying and to stop bystanders from silently condoning it. It may be as simple as implementing an anti-bullying pledge in your classroom (see the Anti-Bullying Pledge on the CD). Consider planning lessons and units around bullying. You may start with Children's Literature Related to Bullying or the many online resources that include specific lesson plans and units (see the CD).

With elementary students' increased access to technology, teachers and parents need to be educated about the dangerous results of cyber bullying, including increased school violence and student suicides. Promote responsible Internet use in the classroom and in school-wide curriculum. Plan and implement lessons to educate students about the dangers of cyber bullying. Invite a liaison from the police department to speak to students and parents about cyber bullying. The parent newsletter is a place to share current articles and resources about bullying and how to stop it. If your school does not have an anti-bullying plan or program, talk to the principal about planning and implementing a school wide program as soon as possible.

> TEACHING TOLERANCE
>
> ## Anti-Bullying Pledge
>
> We the students of _____
> agree to join together to stop bullying.
>
> BY SIGNING THIS PLEDGE I AGREE TO:
> • Treat others respectfully.
> • Try to include those who are left out.
> • Refuse to bully others.
> • Refuse to watch, laugh or join in when someone is being bullied.
> • Tell an adult.
> • Help those who are being bullied.
>
> Signed by
>
> Date

What Experts Say: When bullying continues and a school does not take action, the entire school climate can be affected in the following ways:

- The school develops an environment of fear and disrespect.
- Students have difficulty learning.
- Students feel insecure.
- Students dislike school.
- Students perceive that teachers and staff have little control and don't care about them. (Olweus, 2009, para. #8)

Bullying Resources

Beaudoin, M., & Taylor, M. (2004). Breaking the culture of bullying and disrespect, grades k–8: Best practices and successful strategies. Thousand Oak, CA: Corwin Press.

Espelage, D. L., Bosworth, K., & Simon, T. S. (2001). Short-term stability and change of bullying in middle school students: An examination of demographic, psychosocial, and environmental correlates. *Violence and Victims, 16*(4), 411–426.

Espelage, D. L., & Holt, M. K. (2001). Bullying and victimization during early adolescence: Peer influences and psychosocial correlates (pp. 123–142). Binghamton, NY: Haworth Press.

Espelage, D. L., Holt, M. K., & Henkel, R. R. (in press). Examination of peer group contextual effects on aggression during early adolescence. *Child Development.*

Nansel, T. R., Overpeck, M., Pilla, R. S., Ruan, W. J., Simons-Morton, B., & Scheidt, P. (2001). Bullying behaviors among U.S. youth: Prevalence and association with psychosocial adjustment. *Journal of the American Medical Association, 285*(16), 2094–2100.

Pellegrini, A. D. (2002). Bullying, victimization, and sexual harassment during the transition to middle school. *Educational Psychologist, 37*(3), 151–164.

Rodkin, P. C., Farmer, T. W., Pearl, R., & Van Acker, R. (2000). Heterogeneity of popular boys: Antisocial and prosocial configurations. *Developmental Psychology, 36*(1), 14–24.

Rudolph, K. D., Lambert, S. F., Clark, A. G., & Kurlakowsky, K. D. (2001). Negotiating the transition to middle school: The role of self-regulatory processes. *Child Development, 72*(3), 929–946.

Online Resources

Dealing with Bullying (KidsHealth):
http://kidshealth.org/teen/your_mind/problems/bullies.html

It's My Life (PBS Kids): http://pbskids.org/itsmylife/friends/bullies/

Prevention and Control:
http://www.safeyouth.org/scripts/topics/bullying.asp

Safe Youth: Bullying (National Youth Violence Prevention Resource Center sponsored by the Centers for Disease Control and Prevention): http://www.safeyouth.org/scripts/topics/bullying.asp

Stop Bullying Now (United States Department of Health and Human Services): http://stopbullyingnow.hrsa.gov/kids/

Teaching Tolerance: A Project of the Southern Poverty Law Center: http://www.tolerance.org

Online Resources on Cyberbullying

Cyberbully. National Crime Prevention Council:
http://www.ncpc.org/cyberbullying
http://www.mcgruff.org/Advice/cyberbullies.php

e-bullying. Teaching Tolerance: A Project of the Southern Poverty Law Center:
http://www.tolerance.org/teach/magazine/features.jsp?cid=653

Stop Cyber Bullying: http://www.stopcyberbullying.org/index2.html

Conflict Resolution

Conflict is an inevitable part of life. Master teachers recognize that students have disagreements with each other, their families, and their teachers. Conflict resolution is an approach to resolving disagreements between students in a mutually respectful manner. Master teachers keep in mind the values of the school community as they develop a plan for conflict resolution. Conflict resolution may result in students listening to each other, understanding multiple perspectives, and recognizing and accepting differences. The point of conflict resolution is for students to develop interpersonal skills that enable them to independently resolve disagreements without conflict—a life skill.

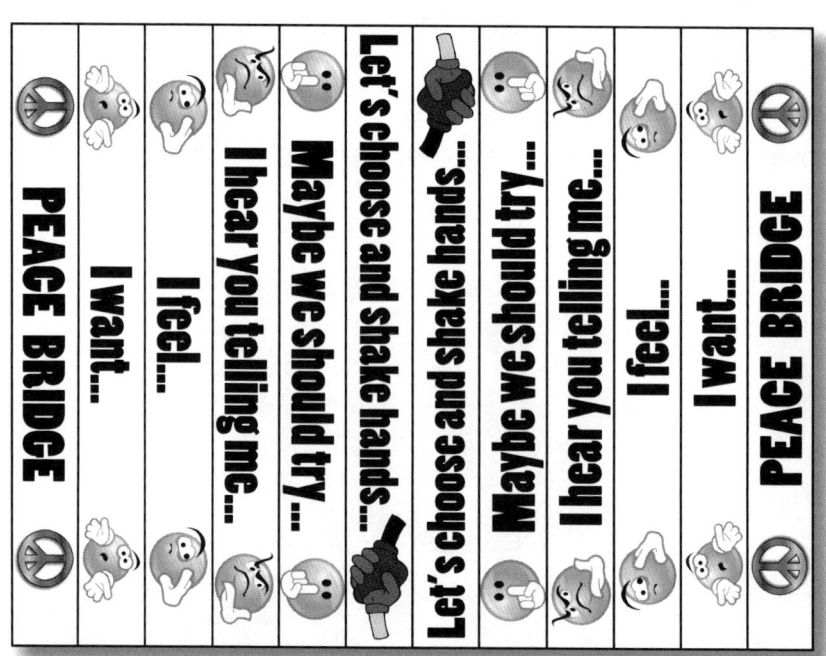

There are many conflict resolution curriculums. Some are complex and involve the entire school, while some are simple and work in a single classroom. Peer mediation, a school-wide approach, is a process in which students facilitate other students' resolution of disputes. Peer mediation programs have been effective in many schools. The Peace Bridge is an example of a simple approach to conflict resolution. Some schools and classrooms use the Peace Bridge as a tool for resolving student disagreements (see the CD). The bridge may be painted on the school playground, gym floor, hallway wall, or even on the floor of the classroom. Two students begin on each side of the Peace Bridge by facing each other on the first step. They take turns explaining what they each want to happen, how they feel, and what they understand about how the other person feels. They think of ways to solve the problem, they choose a solution, and they shake hands. Use role play to practice the Peace Bridge process. Give pairs of students scenarios as practice. Follow up by enlisting all students to share solutions to the scenarios. This process takes some time, but the conflict that will be avoided makes it a good investment.

A good way to integrate conflict resolution into curriculum is to use children's literature. (See Children's Literature Related to Conflict Resolution on the CD.) There are several books that reinforce conflict resolution approaches that can be used for silent reading, read-alouds, and other literacy activities.

Reacting to Volatile Situations

Sometimes students may lose control and present a danger to themselves and/or others. Master teachers react quickly and calmly and may try a variety of tactics depending on the student and the situation. Ask for help immediately whether it is phoning the office, sounding a buzzer, or asking a student to get help from another teacher. Then, get the student's attention and divert the student away from the conflict. Speak to the student using his or her name. Keep your voice firm but not threatening. Avoid turning the situation into a power struggle. Move slowly and deliberately toward the conflict while keeping a short distance between you and the student. If appropriate, tell the student to stop the dangerous behavior. Give the student time to cool down and decide what to do. If the student's behavior escalates into dangerous behavior, put the safety of other students first. Plan in advance where students will go when you use the preplanned signal for students to leave. In most cases, it is better to avoid becoming physically involved yourself. The unintended consequences of putting yourself in danger are personal injury and traumatized students.

Chapter 9
Last Words, Next Steps

Concluding Remarks

Teaching is about the students—from classroom to curriculum. Keeping students in the forefront of everything you do is the key to mastering the art of the elementary classroom. If it's good for kids, do it. Teaching is an ongoing process that one never completely masters because there are always new students, new curriculum, and new research. So while these are our last words for moving from surviving to thriving, following are some next steps to mastering the art of the elementary classroom. Professional growth is dependent upon personal growth; they occur simultaneously. Growth is your personal and professional responsibility. Master teachers are dedicated to new learning, open to revelations, and committed to renewal.

There are a myriad of approaches to contemplate teaching and learning and the context in which those processes occur. Pondering the thoughts of others or reflecting on questions regarding your own thoughts are avenues to growing personally and professionally. New learning transpires from reading books. Revelations occur when quotes resonate within you and reveal new perspectives. Questions push you to examine your beliefs and assumptions. Renewal happens when the passion for teaching and learning is deepened by the participation in activities that facilitate personal and professional growth.

Books that Inspire and Teach

There is no end to books and authors that inspire and teach. The books that follow will provoke thought, conversation, and learning. Read books independently or form a book club in which colleagues agree to read and discuss books together. Ask the principal about starting a book club at your school for professional development. Keep in mind, learning begins with you. When you read a meaningful book, pass it on.

Books We Recommend

Apple, M. W. (2001). *Educating the "right" way: Markets, standards, God, and inequality.* New York: Routledge-Falmer.

Brookfield, S. D. (2005). *The power of critical theory: Liberating adult learning and teaching.* San Francisco: Jossey-Bass.

Brooks, J. G., & Brooks, M. G. (1993). *In search of understanding: The case for constructivist classrooms.* Alexandria, VA: Association for Supervision and Curriculum Development.

Codell, E. R. (2003). *Sahara special.* New York: Scholastic Books.

Esquith, R. (2007). *Teach like your hair's on fire: The methods and madness inside room 56.* New York: Viking.

Esquith, R. (2003). *There are no shortcuts: How an inner-city teacher--winner of the American teacher award—inspires his students and challenges us to rethink the way we educate our children.* New York: Pantheon.

Fuller, R. W. (2003). *Somebodies and nobodies: Overcoming the abuse of rank.* Gabriola Island, B.C., Canada: New Society Publishers.

Gladwell, M. (2008). *Outliers.* New York: Little Brown and Company.

Hart, B., & Risley, T. R. (1995). *Meaningful differences in the everyday experience of young American children.* Baltimore, MD: Paul H. Brookes Publishing Co.

Kohn, A. (1999). *Punished by rewards: The trouble with gold stars, incentive plans, A's, praise, and other bribes.* Boston: Houghton Mifflin.

Kohn, A. (2006). *Beyond discipline: From compliance to community* (2nd ed.). Alexandria, VA: Association for Supervision and Curriculum Development.

Kohn, A. (2006). *The homework myth: Why our kids get too much of a bad thing.* Cambridge, MA: Da Capo Press.

Kozol, J. (1995). *Amazing grace: The lives of children and the conscience of a nation.* New York: Perennial.

Kozol, J. (2005). *The shame of the nation: The restoration of apartheid schooling in America.* New York: Crown Publishers.

Ladson-Billings, G. (1994). *The dreamkeepers: Successful teachers of African American Children.* San Francisco: Jossey-Bass Publishers.

Lawrence-Lightfoot, A. (2003). The *essential conversation: What parents and teachers can learn from each other.* New York: Ballantine Books.

Loeb, P. R. (1999). *Soul of a citizen: Living with conviction in a cynical time.* New York: St. Martin's Griffin.

Marzano, R. J. (2004). *Building background knowledge for academic achievement.* Alexandria, VA: Association for Supervision and Curriculum Development.

Mortenson, G., & Relin, D. O. (2006). *Three cups of tea: One man's mission to promote peace…one school at a time.* New York: Penguin Books.

Pink, D. H. (2006). *A whole new mind: Why right-brainers will rule the future.* New York: Riverhead Books.

Restak, R. (2001). *The new brain: How the modern age is rewiring your mind.* Emmaus, PA: Rodale.

Sharron, H., & Coulter, M. (2004). *Changing children's minds: Feuerstein's revolution in the teaching of intelligence.* Highlands, TX: aha! Process, Inc.

Strobel, R. G. (2005). *A black eye isn't the end of the world: The panda principles.* Kansas City: MO: Andrews McMeel Publishing.

Suskind, R. (1998). *A hope in the unseen: An American odyssey from the inner city to the ivy league.* New York: Broadway Books.

Sylwester, R. (1995). *A celebration of neurons: An educator's guide to the human brain.* Alexandria, VA: Association for Supervision and Curriculum Development.

Sylwester, R. (2003). *A biological brain in a cultural classroom* (2nd ed.). Thousand Oaks, CA: Corwin Press, Inc.

Wheatley, M. J. (2002). *Turning to one another: Simple conversations to restore hope to the future.* San Francisco: Berrett-Koehler Publishers, Inc.

Willis, J. (2006). *Research-based strategies to ignite student learning: Insights from a neurologist and classroom teacher.* Alexandria, VA: Association for Supervision and Curriculum Development.

Inspirational Quotes to Contemplate and Share

Use quotes to stimulate your own and others' thinking. As you are reading, write down quotes that make powerful statements. Share quotes with your colleagues, students, and parents. Add them to an agenda, email, or newsletter. Create mini-posters of quotes for the classroom, school hallways, or staff lounge. Use inspirational quotes on bookmarks to give to students. Start a collection of quotes.

The chief source of the problem of discipline in schools is that...a premium is put on physical quietude; on silence, on rigid uniformity of posture and movement; upon a machine-like simulation of the attitudes of intelligent interest. The teachers' business is to hold the pupils up to these requirements and to punish the inevitable deviations which occur.
—John Dewey, Philosopher and Educator

It is in most respects a teacher-directed model, one in which expectations, rules, and consequences are imposed on students. And it is typically driven by a remarkably negative set of beliefs about the nature of children. But whenever things go wrong in such classrooms—which is often—the approach itself is rarely blamed. It is the children who are said to be incorrigible, or the teachers who are faulted for being insufficiently firm or skillful.
—Alfie Kohn, Author and Advocate for Children

The mediocre teacher tells. The good teacher explains. The superior teacher demonstrates. The great teacher inspires.
—William Arthur Ward, British novelist

You want to raise the expectations of your students, but first you have to raise your expectations of yourself.

—Robyn Jackson, Writer

Our aspirations are our possibilities.

—Robert Browning, Poet

I now see my life, not as the slow shaping of achievements to fit my preconceived purposes, but as the gradual discovery of a purpose which I did not know.

—Joanna Field, Writer

Do what you can, with what you have, where you are.

—Theodore Roosevelt, U. S. President

Act as if what you do makes a difference. It does.

—William James, Author

Quality is not just a chart, or a standard, or a specification—it's a state of mind, a commitment, a responsibility, a spirit. It's a way of doing, being and living.

—Don Galer, Author

When we put a limit on what we will do, we put a limit on what we can do.

—Charles Schwab, Business Expert

When you do the best you can, you never know what miracle is wrought in your life, or in the life of another.

—Helen Keller, Teacher, Author, and Activist

There's always one moment in life when the door opens and lets the future in.

—Graham Green, Author, Playwright, and Literary Critic

The best minute you spend is the one you invest in people.
—Ken Blanchard, Business Expert

We must have places where children can have a whole group of adults they can trust.
—Margaret Mead, Anthropologist

The future is in the hands of those who can give tomorrow's generations valid reasons to live and hope.
—Teilhard de Chardin, Author

Treat people as if they were what they ought to be and you help them to become what they are capable of being.
—Johann Wolfgang von Goethe, Philosopher, Playwright

You can work miracles by expressing faith in others. To get the best out of people, choose to think and believe the best about them.
—Bob Moawad, Author

There is more hunger for love and appreciation in this world than for bread.
—Mother Teresa, Humanitarian

He drew a circle that shut me out—
Heretic, rebel, a thing to flout.
But love and I had the wit to win;
We drew a circle that took him in.
—Edwin Markham, Poet

Seven national crimes: I don't think. I don't know. I don't care. I am too busy. I leave well enough alone. I have no time to read and find out. I am not interested.
—William Boetcker, Religious Leader

The difference between what we do and what we are capable of doing would solve most of the world's problems.
—Mahatma Gandhi, World Leader

I am only one, but still I am one. I cannot do everything, but still I can do something. And because I cannot do everything, I will not refuse to do the something that I can do.
—Helen Keller, Teacher, Author, and Activist

Nobody ever has it all together. That's like trying to eat once and for all.
—Marilyn Grey, Humorist

Organizing is what you do before you do something, so that when you do it, it is not all mixed up.
—A. A. Milne, Author

Out of intense complexities intense simplicities emerge.
—Winston Churchill, World Leader

They may forget what you said but they will never forget how you made them feel.
—Carl W. Buechner, Author

Keep in mind that your students will remember only some of what you taught them but everything about how they felt in your classroom.
—Mara Sapon-Shevin, Profesosor of Inclusive Education, Syracuse University

Knowing others is wisdom, knowing yourself is enlightenment
—Lao Tzu, Chinese Philosopher

Follow effective action with quiet reflection. From the quiet reflection will come even more effective action.
—Peter F. Drucker, Father of Modern Management

Sometimes questions are more important than answers.
— Nancy Willard, Poet

Time for reflection with colleagues is for me a lifesaver; it is not just a nice thing to do if you have the time. It is the only way you can survive.
— Margaret Wheatley, Author and Management Consultant

Our deepest fear is not that we are inadequate. Our deepest fear is that we are powerful beyond measure. It is our Light, not our Darkness, that most frightens us. We ask ourselves, Who am I to be brilliant, gorgeous, talented, fabulous? Actually, who are you not to be?
— Marianne Williamson, Author

All children could and should be inventors of their own theories, critics of other people's ideas, analyzers of evidence, and makers of their own personal marks on this most complex world.
— Deborah Meier, Educator and Author

Since there is no single set of abilities running throughout human nature, there is no single curriculum which all should undergo. Rather, the schools should teach everything that anyone is interested in learning.
— John Dewey, Philosopher and Educator

I have always believed that I could help change the world, because I have been lucky to have adults around me who did.
— Marian Wright Edelman, Advocate for Children

Children have never been very good at listening to their elders, but they have never failed to imitate them.
— James Baldwin

Even when we can't envision the ideal future, we can still recognize callousness, shortsightedness, and injustice. And we can still challenge it with compassion, vision, and courage.
— Paul Rogut Loeb, Author

A good society also helps each of us fulfill the full bloom of our uniqueness. It honors our individual gifts and encourages our particular callings. It gives all its inhabitants the economic, emotional, and spiritual support needed to follow their dreams. An unjust one, in contrast, starves hopes, aspirations, and possibilities. It stunts lives and potentials.
—Paul Rogut Loeb, Author

The time has come to lower our voices, to cease imposing our mechanistic patterns on the biological processes of the earth, to resist the impulse to control, to command, to force, to oppress, and to begin quite humbly to follow the guidance of the larger community on which all life depends. Our fulfillment is not in our isolated human grandeur, but in our intimacy with the larger earth community, for this is also the larger dimension of our being. Our human destiny is integral with the destiny of the earth.
—Thomas Berry, Historian

The unexamined life is not worth living.
—Socrates, Greek Philosopher

Everything should be made as simple as possible, but not one bit simpler.
—Albert Einstein, Scientist

Life isn't about finding yourself. Life is about creating yourself.
—George Bernard Shaw, Writer

Questions for Reflection and Dialogue

Classrooms exist within a larger context and are not isolated from the bigger issues that impact society. Thought-provoking questions facilitate reflection and dialogue, and they may lead to action. Asking the right question may be more important than finding the right answer. And, trying to answer one question usually leads to more questions. In any case, let the following questions guide your reflection and conversation with colleagues.

- What are your assumptions behind beliefs you hold about teaching, learning, and/or students?
- Are all students receiving the same quality of instruction?
- Is every student valued for the contributions he or she can make in the future and taught with that future in mind?
- How can I build community in my classroom if I do not accept every student?
- How can I prevent bullying behaviors if I do not respect every child's uniqueness?
- What do I believe about children?
- What do I believe the purpose of education is?
- What do I believe children should learn in school?
- What do I believe about democratic classrooms?
- What do I believe about standardized testing?
- What do I believe about constructivism and student-centered teaching?
- What is my definition of a master teacher?
- What are my strengths that relate to being a master teacher?
- What are my opportunities for growth?
- What am I willing to do to promote quality education for every child?

Renewal

Renewal is a process to rekindle your passion and replenish your energy. The intent of renewal is to increase your capacity for teaching and learning. Your students' learning is connected to your learning. Master teachers take time to take care of themselves, feed their intellectual spirit, and perfect their craft. Fullan and Hargreaves (1991-1993) suggest the following guidelines for teachers seeking professional growth:

- Locate, listen to, and articulate your inner voice.
- Practice reflection in action, on action, and about action.
- Develop a risk-taking mentality.
- Trust processes as well as people.
- Appreciate the total person in working with others.
- Commit to working with colleagues.
- Seek variety and avoid balkanization.
- Redefine your role to extend beyond the classroom.
- Balance work and life.
- Push and support principals and other administrators to develop interactive professionalism.
- Commit to continuous improvement and perpetual learning.
- Monitor and strengthen the connection between your development and students'

Bibliography

Bacon, L. (1994). It's about time! A report from the national education association's special committee on time resources (ERIC) Document Reproduction Service, No. ED 4582000.

Barth, R. (2006). Improving relationships within the school house. *Educational Leadership, 63*(6), 13.

Beaudoin, M., & Taylor, M. (2004). *Breaking the culture of bullying and disrespect, grades K–8.* Thousand Oaks, CA: Corwin Press.

Borek, J., & Parsons, S. (2004). *Research on improving teacher time management.* Academic Exchange Quarterly. Retrieved April 7, 2009, from the BNET Web site: http://www.findarticles.com/p/articles/mi_hb3325/is_3_8/ai_n29144383/pg_4?tag=content;coll

Brewer. C. B. (2009). *Music and learning: Integrating music in the classroom.* Retrieved April 24, 2009, from New Horizons for Learning Web site: http://www.newhorizons.org/strategies/arts/brewer.htm

Brookhart, S. (2008). *How to give effective feedback to your students.* Alexandria, VA: Association for Supervision and Curriculum Development.

Carneiro, P., & Heckman, J. J. (2002). *Human capital policy.* Paper presented at the Alvin Hansen Seminar, Harvard University, Cambridge, MA.

The Center on School, Family, and Community Partnerships at Johns Hopkins University, (2006). *Teachers involve parents in homework.* Retrieved March 21, 2009, from the National Network of Partnership Schools, Johns Hopkins University Web site: http://www.csos.jhu.edu/P2000/tips/index.htm

Chappuis, S., Chappuis, J., & Stiggins, R. (2009). Supporting Teacher Learning Teams. *Educational Leadership*, 66(5), 13.

Collinson, V., & Cook, T.F. (2000). *"I don't have enough time": Teacher's interpretations of time as a key to learning and school change.* Michigan; US (ERIC No. ED 446038)

Denton, P. (2008). The power of our words. *Educational Leadership*, 66 (1), 28.

Education World (2009). Parents Involved in Schools. Retrieved March 21, 2009, from the Education World Web site: http://www.educationworld.com/a_special/parent_involvement.shtml

Emmer. E. T., Evertson, C.M., & Worsham, M.E. (2003). *Classroom management for secondary teachers* (6th ed). Boston: Allyn & Bacon.

Epstein, J. L. (2003). Foreword. In E. N. Patrikakou, R. P. Weissberg, S. Redding, & H. J. Walberg (Eds.), *School-family partnerships for children's success* (pp. vii–xi). New York: Teachers College Press.

Epstein, J., & Dawber, S. (1991). School programs and teacher practices of parent involvement in inner-city elementary and middle schools. *The Elementary School Journal*, 91(3), 289.

Evertson, C., & Weinstein, C. (2006). Handbook of classroom management. Mahwah, NJ: Lawrence Erlbaum Associates.

Fullan & Hargreaves, 1991-1993. See msp. 151.

Greene, P. K., & Tichenor, M. S. (2003). Parents and schools: No stopping the involvement! *Childhood Education*, 79, 242–243.

Henderson, A. T., & Mapp, K. L. (2002). *A new wave of evidence: The impact of school, family and community connections on student achievement.* Austin, TX: National Center for Family and Community Connections with Schools.

Kohn, A. (2006). *Beyond discipline: From compliance to community* (10th anniversary ed.). Alexandria, VA: Association for Supervision of Curriculum and Development.

Marzano, R., Gaddy, B., Foseid, M. C., Foseid, M. P., & Marzano, J. (2005). *A Handbook for Classroom Management that Works.* Upper Saddle River, NJ: Merrill Education, ASCD College Textbook Series.

Bibliography

Marzano, R. J., Marzano, J. S., & Pickering, D. J. (2003). *Classroom Management that Works Research-Based Strategies for Every Teacher.* Alexandria, VA: Association for Supervision of Curriculum and Development.

McLeod, J., Fisher, J., & Hoover, G. (2003). *The key elements of classroom management: Managing time and space, student behavior, and instructional strategies summary.* Alexandria, VA: Association for Supervision of Curriculum and Development.

Metlife, (2008). *A Survey of Teachers, Principals, and Students.* Retrieved March 12, 2009, from http://www.michigan.gov/documents/Guide_to_Home_Visits_44583_7.pdf

Michigan Department of Education. (1999). A Guide to Home Visits. Retrieved March 12, National Middle School Association. (2003). *This we believe: Successful schools for young adolescents.* Westerville, OH: Author.

Oleweus, D. (2009). What is Bullying? Retrieved May 9, 2009, from the OLWESU Bullying Prevention Program Web site: http://www.olweus.org/public/bullying.page

Sapon-Shevin, M. (2008). Learning in an inclusive community. *Educational Leadership, 66*(1), 51.

Sensory Integration Disorder, (2009). *Problem behavior in the classroom: Dealing with children and sensory processing disorders at school.* Retrieved April 24, 2009, from the Sensory Processing Disorder Web site: http://www.sensory-processing-disorder.com/problem-behavior-in-the-classroom.html

Thompson, N. (2002), *People Skills.* Hampshire, UK: Palgrave Macmillan.

WCCO-TV, (2009). *Education: standing desks.* Retrieved April 24, 2009, from the WCCO Web site: http://wcco.com/education/stand.up.desks.2.566063.html

Weigal, D., Behal, P., & Martin, S. (2001). The family storyteller: A collaborative family collaborative literacy program. *Journal of Extension, 39* (4), 1.

Werderich, D. (2008). Bringing family and community into the writing curriculum. *Middle School Journal, 39*(3), 34.

Wiebke, K., & Bardin, J. (2009, Winter). New teacher support. *Journal of Staff Development, 30*(1), 34–38.

WittFitt, (2009). *Kids on the move: Stability balls.* Retrieved April 24, 2009, from the WittFitt Web site: http://www.wittfitt.com/index.htm

Appendix
CD Contents

Chapter 1: Rest, Reflect, Renew
1. Checklist—Home Visits
2. Checklist—Last Week of School
3. Checklist—Month Before School Starts
4. Checklist—Week Before School Starts
5. Checklist for New Teachers or New Positions
6. Checklist for Summer—Personal
7. Checklist for Summer—Professional

Chapter 2: First Contact with Parents
1. Before School Starts Parent Letter
2. Before School Starts Student Postcard
3. Before School Starts Student Letter
4. Family Handbook
5. First Week of School Letter
6. Help Wanted Form
7. Class Newsletter Sample
8. Parent Questionnaire

Chapter 3: Partnering with Parents
1. Family Homework Assignment Form
2. Family Homework Calendar
3. Family Homework Letter
4. Learning Centers and Stations
5. Parent Information Night (PIN) Handout
6. PowerPoint Presentation for PIN

Chapter 4: Engaging in School Culture
1. Classroom Activities for Substitute Teachers
2. Letter for Substitute
3. Read-Aloud Lesson for Substitute
4. Substitute Feedback Form
5. Substitute Folder Checklist
6. Traveling Student Log
7. Video Activity 1
8. Video Activity 2

Chapter 5: It's About Time
1. Family Calendar
2. Take-Home Folder Check-Off List
3. Task List
4. While You Were Absent

Chapter 6: Space Strategies
None

Chapter 7: Building Relationships with Students
1. Alphabet Squares
2. Class Bill of Rights Lesson
3. Classroom Classmate Bingo
4. Classroom Job Application Form
5. First Morning Tasks
6. Game On!

7. Getting to Know Your Students PowerPoint Slides
8. Introducing Yourself to Students PowerPoint
9. Inventories—Reading, Writing, and Math
10. Literature for the First Days of School
11. Me in a Bag Activity and Parent Letter
12. Sign the Brick Wall
13. Student Interview Activity
14. Student Search
15. Team Statistics—Group
16. Team Statistics—Individual

Bonus Material on CD
17. Baseball Theme Activities and Materials
18. Classroom Quilt Lesson Plan
19. Crayon Box Lesson Plan with Crayon Template
20. If You're Looking for…
21. My Favorite Is!
22. Questions to Prompt Critical Thinking

Chapter 8: Responding to Student Behavior
1. Children's Literature Related to Bullying
2. Children's Literature Related to Conflict Resolution
3. Peace Bridge
4. Problem-Solving Process—Student Handout
5. Teaching Tolerance Anti-Bullying Pledge

Chapter 9: Last Words, Next Steps
None

About the Authors

Linda L. Carpenter, M. Ed.

Linda Carpenter has a B.A. in History and completed her Master's of Education degree with a concentration in Educational Technology at Cardinal Stritch University, Milwaukee, Wisconsin. In addition to having taught both social studies and language arts, Linda served as Technology Integration Specialist for 4K-5 schools. Linda teaches in the Master of Arts in Teaching program at Cardinal Stritch University. In addition to her work with pre-service teacher candidates, she has extensive experience both in teaching and staff development in K-12 schools and teacher certification in four states.

Jennifer J. Fontanini, Ed. D.

Dr. Jennifer Fontanini is an Assistant Professor in the College of Education and Leadership at Cardinal Stritch University and has a B.S. in Secondary Education, Master's in curriculum and instruction, and a doctorate in education leadership. Previously, Jennifer taught middle school and high school social studies and designed an integrated curriculum for social studies and language arts. She teaches in the Master of Arts in Teaching program at Cardinal Stritch University where her focus is research-based methodologies of instruction and assessment.

Linda V. Neiman, Ph. D.

Dr. Linda Neiman has a B.A. in English, a Master's degree in literacy, and a doctorate in Leadership for the Advancement of Service and Learning. She has taught English/Language Arts in grades 5-12 and served as a Reading Specialist and Professional Development Specialist in a variety of K-12 schools in southeastern Wisconsin. Currently Linda teaches in the Masters of Arts in Teaching program at Cardinal Stritch University, Milwaukee, Wisconsin, where her research is focused on best practice implementation in K-12 classroom.